Most Lawyers Are Lai

The Truth About Taxes

Written by

Money Guy and Tax Guy

Congratulations! Your business is earning money and it is time to do your taxes. What you are not told is the more you make the more you pay. You worked hard, lost sleep, made sacrifices, missed family trips, worked every day for three years, and now you are a millionaire, or just made your first $100,000. Either way the IRS does not care, in fact they want you to make more so they can tax you more. It is like your being punished for working them long unpaid hours in life, that you will never get back. All in the name of wanting to do better for your family. Well, there is some good news, the tax codes if you know how to use them, will help you lessen your taxes. Get you a good CPA that is willing to use all codes in your favor, some CPAs see the tax season as a sport. They get off on helping their clients not pay as much in taxes. Get that guy/girl.

With that said, let us see what taxes is all about.

What Are Taxes?

Taxes are mandatory contributions levied on individuals or corporations by a government entity—whether local, regional, or national. Tax revenues finance government activities, including public works and services such as roads and schools, or programs such as Social Security and Medicare. In economics, taxes fall on whomever pays the burden of the tax, whether this is the entity being taxed, such as a business, or the end consumers of the business's goods.

From an accounting perspective, there are various taxes to consider, including payroll taxes, federal and state income taxes, and sales taxes.

Key Takeaways

- Taxes are mandatory contributions collected by governments.

- The Internal Revenue Service (IRS) collects federal income taxes in the United States.

- There are many forms of taxes; most are applied as a percentage of a monetary exchange (for example, when income is earned, or a sales transaction is completed).

- Other forms of taxes, such as property taxes, are applied based on the assessed value of a held asset.

- Understanding what triggers, a tax situation can enable taxpayers to manage their finances to minimize the impact of taxes.

Understanding Taxes

To help fund public works and services—and to build and maintain the infrastructure used in a country—a government usually taxes its individual and corporate residents.1 The tax collected is used for the betterment of the economy and all who are living in it. In the United States and many other countries in the world, income taxes are applied to some form of money received by a taxpayer. The money could be income earned from salary, capital gains from investment appreciation, dividends or interest received as additional income, payment made for goods and services, etc.

Tax revenues are used for public services and the operation of the government, as well as for

Social Security and Medicare. As baby boomer populations have aged, Social Security and Medicare have claimed increasingly high proportions of the total federal expenditure of tax revenue. Throughout U.S. history, tax policy has been a consistent source of political debate.

A tax requires a percentage of the taxpayer's earnings or money to be taken and remitted to the government. Payment of taxes at rates levied by the government is compulsory, and tax evasion—the deliberate failure to pay one's full tax liabilities—is punishable by law. (On the other hand, tax avoidance—actions taken to lessen your tax liability and maximize after-tax income—is perfectly legal.) Most governments use an agency or department to collect taxes. In the United States, this function is performed federally by the Internal Revenue Service (IRS).

There are several quite common types of taxes:

- Income tax—a percentage of generated income that is relinquished to the state or federal government

- Payroll tax—a percentage withheld from an employee's pay by an employer, who pays it to the government on the employee's behalf to fund Medicare and Social Security programs

- Corporate tax—a percentage of corporate profits taken as tax by the government to fund federal programs

- Sales tax—taxes levied on certain goods and services; varies by jurisdiction

- Property tax—based on the value of land and property assets

- Tariff—taxes on imported goods; imposed in the aim of strengthening internal businesses

- Estate tax—rate applied to the reasonable value of property in a person's estate at the time of death; total estate must exceed thresholds set by state and federal governments

Tax systems vary widely among nations, and it is important for individuals and corporations to carefully study a new locale's tax laws before earning income or doing business there.

Below, we will look at various tax situations in the United States. The federal government levies income, corporate, and payroll taxes; the state levies income and sales taxes; and municipalities or other local governments levy property taxes.

Income tax

Like many nations, the United States has a progressive income tax system, through which a higher percentage of tax revenues are collected from high-income individuals or corporations than from low-income individual earners. Taxes are applied through marginal tax rates.

A variety of factors affect the marginal tax rate that a taxpayer will pay, including their filing status—married filing jointly, married filing separately, single, or head of household. Which status a person files can make a significant difference in how much they are taxed. The source of a taxpayer's income also makes a difference in taxation. It is important to learn the terminology of the different income types that may affect how income is taxed.

Capital gains taxes are of relevance for investors. Levied and enforced at the federal level, these are taxes on income from the sale of assets in which the sale price was higher than the purchasing price. These are taxed at both short- and long-term rates. Short-term capital gains (on assets sold one year or less after they were acquired) are taxed at the owner's ordinary income tax rate, but long-term gains on assets held for more than a year are taxed at a lower capital gains rate, on the rationale that lower taxes will encourage elevated levels of capital investment. Tax records should be maintained to substantiate the length of ownership when both the assets were sold, and the tax return was filed.

Payroll taxes

Payroll taxes are withheld from an employee's paycheck by an employer, who remits the amount to the federal government to fund Medicare and Social Security programs. Employees pay 6.2% into Social Security on the first $142,800 earned (the wage base limit for 2021) and 1.45% into Medicare on all wages. Because there is a cap on wages subject to the Social Security portion of the payroll tax, it is regressive, with higher-paid earners paying a smaller percentage of their total wages.

There is no salary limit for Medicare tax, but anyone who earns more than $200,000 as a single filer (or $250,000 for married couples filing jointly) pays an additional 0.9% into Medicare.

Payroll taxes have both an employee portion and an employer portion. The employer remits both the employee portion, described above, and a duplicate amount for the employer portion. The employer rates are the same 6.2% for Social Security, up to the wage base limit, and 1.45% for Medicare on all wages. Therefore, the total remitted is 15.3% (6.2% employee Social Security + 6.2% employer Social Security + 1.45% employee Medicare + 1.45% employer Medicare).

Payroll taxes and income taxes differ, although both are withheld from an employee's paycheck and remitted to the government. Payroll taxes are specifically to fund Social Security and Medicare programs. A self-employed individual must pay the equivalent of both the employee and employer portion of payroll taxes through self-employment taxes, which also fund Social Security and Medicare.

Corporate taxes

Corporate taxes are paid on a company's taxable income. The steps to calculate a company's taxable income are:

- Sales revenue - cost of goods sold (COGS) = gross profit

- Gross profit - operating expenses (such as general and administrative expenses (G&A), selling and marketing, research and development (R&D), depreciation, etc.) = earnings before interest and taxes (EBIT)

- EBIT - interest expense = taxable income

The corporate tax rate in the United States is currently a flat rate of 21%. Before the Tax Cuts and Jobs Act (TCJA) of 2017, the corporate tax rate was 35%.

Sales taxes

Sales taxes are charged at the point of sale, when a customer executes the payment for a good or service. The business collects the sales tax from the customer and remits the funds to the government. Different jurisdictions charge different sales taxes, which often overlap, as when states, counties, and municipalities each levy their own sales taxes.

As of 2021, the highest average state and local sales tax rate is found in Tennessee, at 9.55%. Five states do not have a state sales tax: Alaska, Delaware, Montana, New Hampshire, and Oregon. Alaska does allow municipalities to charge local sales tax.

Property taxes

A common property tax in the United States is the real estate ad valorem tax. A millage rate is used to calculate real estate taxes; it represents the amount per every $1,000 of a property's assessed value. The property's assessed value is determined by a property assessor appointed by the local government. Reassessments are typically performed every one to five years. Property tax rates vary by jurisdiction. Property taxes can also be assessed on private property, such as cars or boats.

As of 2018, the state with the highest property tax collections per capita was New Jersey at $3,378. (The District of Columbia would rank higher if it were counted with the 50 states, at $3,740 per capita.) The lowest state ranking was $598 per capita in Alabama.

Tariffs

A tariff is a tax imposed by one country on the goods and services imported from another country.18 The purpose is to encourage domestic purchases by increasing the price of goods and services imported from other countries.

There are two main types of tariffs: fixed fee tariffs, which are levied as a fixed cost based on the type of item, and ad valorem tariffs, which are assessed as a percentage of the item's value (like the real estate tax in the previous section).

Tariffs are politically divisive, with debate over whether the policies work as intended.

Estate taxes

Estate taxes are levied only on estates that exceed the exclusion limit set by law. In 2021, the federal exclusion limit is $11.7 million. Surviving spouses are exempt from estate taxes. The estate tax due is the taxable estate minus the exclusion limit. For example, a $14.7 million estate would owe estate taxes on $3 million.

The estate tax rate is a progressive marginal rate that increases drastically from 18% to 40%. The maximum estate tax rate of 40% is levied on the portion of an estate that exceeds the exclusion limit by more than $1 million.

States may have lower exclusion limits than the federal government, but no state taxes estates less than $1 million. Massachusetts and Oregon have the $1 million exemption limits. State rates are also different from the federal rate. The highest top state estate tax rates are in Hawaii and Washington, each at 20%.

Estate taxes are different from inheritance taxes, in that an estate tax is applied before assets are disbursed to any beneficiaries. The beneficiary pays an inheritance tax. There is no federal inheritance tax, and only six states have an inheritance tax: Iowa, Kentucky, Maryland, Nebraska, New Jersey, and Pennsylvania.

The Bottom Line

There are many types of taxes that are applied in many ways. Understanding what triggers, a tax situation can enable taxpayers to manage their finances to minimize the impact of taxes. Techniques that can help include annual tax-loss harvesting, to offset investing gains with investing losses, and estate planning, which works to shelter inherited income for heirs.

Head of Household (HOH)

What Is Head of Household (HOH)?

Taxpayers may file tax returns as head of household (HOH) if they pay more than half the cost of supporting and housing a qualifying person. Taxpayers eligible to classify themselves as an HOH get higher standard deductions and lower tax rates than taxpayers who file as single or married filing separately.

Key Takeaways

- To qualify for head of household tax filing status, you must file a separate individual tax return, be considered unmarried, and be entitled to an exemption for a qualifying person.

- The qualifying person must be either a child or parent of the head of household.

- The head of household must pay for more than one-half of the qualifying person's support and housing costs.

Understanding Head of Household

HOH is a filing status available to taxpayers who meet certain qualifying thresholds. They must file separate individual tax returns, be considered unmarried, and be entitled to an exemption for a qualifying person, such as a child or parent. Further, the HOH must pay more than one-half the cost of supporting the qualifying person and more than one-half the cost of maintaining that qualifying person's primary home.

To be considered unmarried, the HOH must be single, divorced, or regarded as unmarried. For example, married taxpayers would be regarded as unmarried if they did not live with their spouse during the last six months of the tax year. The status is further reliant on the HOH meeting either of these two requirements:

☐ The HOH is married to a nonresident alien whom they elect not to treat as a resident alien.

☐ The HOH is legally separated under a divorce or separate maintenance decree by the last day of the tax year.

An HOH must pay for more than one-half of the cost of a qualifying person's support and housing costs. The HOH must also pay more than one-half of the rent or mortgage, utilities, repairs, insurance, taxes, and other costs of maintaining the home where the qualifying person lives for more than half of the year. The home must be the taxpayer's own home, unless the qualifying person is the taxpayer's parent, and the home is the property of that parent.

Since the Tax Cuts and Jobs Act of 2017 (TCJA), the personal exemption has been suspended through 2025. Back when there was one, HOH filers had to be able to claim an exemption for their qualifying person. Taxpayers could release their exemption to a noncustodial parent in a divorce proceeding or a legal separation agreement and remain eligible to file as an HOH.

Married taxpayers are nevertheless considered unmarried if they have not lived with their spouse for the last six months of the tax year.

Examples of Filing as Head of Household

Filing as an HOH can provide significant savings for taxpayers. The 2019 and 2020 tax rate for individuals earning $50,000 and filing as an HOH is 12%. Compare the tax burden shown below for an individual earning $50,000 using the different filing statuses.

Filing as an HOH, the individual will pay 10% of $14,100, or $1,410, plus 12% of the amount over $14,100 ($35,900 × 12% = $4,308), for a total tax of $5,718.

A taxpayer filing single or married filing separately will pay 10% of the first $9,875, or $987.50, plus 12% of $40,125 - $9,875, or $3,630, plus 22% of $50,000 - $40,125, or $2,172.50. This brings the total tax to $987.50 + $3,630 + $2,172.50 = $6,790.

Thus, filing as an HOH saved this hypothetical taxpayer $1,072.

Married Filing Jointly

What Is Married Filing Jointly?

Married filing jointly refers to a filing status for married couples that have wed before the end of the tax year. When filing taxes under married filing jointly status, a married couple can record their respective incomes, deductions, credits, and exemptions on the same tax return.

Married filing jointly is often best if only one spouse has a significant income. However, if both spouses work and the income and itemized deductions are large and very unequal, it may be more advantageous to file separately.

Key Takeaways

- Married filing jointly is an income tax filing status available to any couple that has wed as of Dec. 31 of the tax year.

- It is best used by couples that have one spouse who earns significantly more money than the other.

- It allows a couple to use only one tax return, but both spouses are equally responsible for the return and any taxes and penalties owed.

Should Married Taxpayers File Together?

Understanding Married Filing Jointly

When using married filing jointly filing status, both spouses are equally responsible for the return and the taxes. If either one of the spouses understates the taxes due, both are equally liable for the penalties, unless the other spouse is shown to be unaware of the mistake and did not benefit from it. Taxes can get technical and tricky, so if a couple is having trouble determining tax liability, talk to an experienced tax preparer.

Married Filing Jointly vs. Filing Separately

When using married filing jointly status, your total combined tax liability is often lower than the sum of your and your spouse's individual tax liabilities if you were filing separately. This is because the standard deduction may be higher, and married filing jointly status may qualify for other tax benefits that do not apply to the other filing statuses. (Watch the video for some specifics on these potential benefits.)

A joint tax return will often provide a bigger tax refund or a lower tax liability. However, this is not always the case. A couple may want to investigate their options by calculating the refund or balance due for filing jointly and separately and use the one that provides the biggest refund or the lowest tax liability.

You can use the married filing jointly status if both of the following statements are true:

1. You were married on the last day of the tax year. In other words, if you were married on Dec. 31, then you are considered to have been married all year. If you were unmarried, divorced, or legally separated (according to state law) on Dec. 31, then you are considered unmarried for the year. There is an exception to this rule for the death of a spouse.

2. You and your spouse both agree to file a joint tax return.

A married couple can still be considered unmarried for tax purposes if they meet certain conditions, including having lived apart for the last six months of the tax year.

Also, if you were not divorced or legally separated on Dec. 31, you are considered unmarried if all the following apply:

- You lived apart from your spouse for the last six months of the tax year (not including temporary absences for reasons such as business, medical care, school, or military service).

- You file a separate tax return from your spouse.

- You paid over half the cost of keeping up your home during the tax year.

- Your home was the main home of your child, stepchild, or foster child for more than half of the tax year.

Married Filing Separately

What Is Married Filing Separately?

Married filing separately is a tax status for married couples who choose to record their respective incomes, exemptions, and deductions on separate tax returns. There is a potential tax advantage to filing separately when one spouse has significant medical expenses or miscellaneous itemized deductions, or when both spouses have about the same amount of income.

The alternative to married filing separately is married filing jointly.

Due to the tax law changes that went into effect in 2018, the only time when a couple would gain any advantage from filing separately is if one spouse has significant miscellaneous deductions or medical expenses.

Key Takeaways

- Married filing separately is a tax status used by married couples who choose to record their incomes, exemptions, and deductions on separate tax returns.

- In some circumstances, filing separately puts a couple in a lower tax bracket.

- Although some couples might benefit from filing separately, they may not be able to take advantage of certain tax benefits.

Understanding Married Filing Separately

The Internal Revenue Service (IRS) gives taxpayers five tax filing status options when they submit their annual tax returns: single, married filing jointly, married filing separately, head of household, or qualifying widow(er).

Anyone who files as married in either category—filing separately or filing jointly—must be married as of the last day of the tax year. So, someone who filed taxes for the year 2020 as married must have been married no later than Dec. 31, 2020.

Using the married filing separately status may be appealing and offer financial advantages to certain couples. Combining incomes and filing jointly might push them into a higher tax bracket and thus increase their tax bill.

Although there are financial advantages to filing separately, couples miss tax credits meant for couples who file jointly.

When couples file separately, the IRS requires taxpayers to include their spouse's information on their returns. According to the IRS, if you and your spouse file separate returns and one of you itemizes deductions, then the other spouse will have a standard deduction of zero. Therefore, the other spouse should also itemize deductions.

Note that thanks to the Tax Cuts and Jobs Act (TCJA) of 2017, the standard deduction rose in the 2018 tax year. For 2020 taxes filed in 2021, it climbed again to $12,400 for individuals and $24,800 for married couples filing jointly. As a result of this change, one spouse must have significant miscellaneous deductions or medical expenses for the couple to gain any advantage from filing separately.

Married Filing Separately vs. Married Filing Jointly

Married filing jointly offers the most tax savings, especially when spouses have different income levels. If you use the married filing separately status, then you are unable to take advantage of a number of potentially valuable tax breaks. Some important breaks include:

- Child and Dependent Care Credit. This is a nonrefundable tax credit used by taxpayers to claim unreimbursed childcare expenses. Childcare can include fees paid for babysitters, daycare, summer camps—provided they are not overnight—and other care providers for children under the age of 13 or anyone who cares for dependents of any age who are not physically or mentally able to care for themselves.

The Child and Dependent Care Credit will be more generous in 2021 only, because of the American Rescue Plan. The 2021 credit is 50% of eligible expenses up to a limit based on income. That makes the credit worth up to $4,000 for an individual and up to $8,000 for two or more. The law also increases the exclusion for employer-provided dependent care assistance to $10,500 for 2021.

- American Opportunity Tax Credit (AOTC). Introduced in 2009, the AOTC requires that couples filing jointly have a modified adjusted gross income (MAGI) of no more than $160,000 to be eligible for full credit. Couples who make $160,000 to $180,000, meanwhile, can apply for a partial AOTC. The maximum reward is an annual credit of $2,500 on qualified educational expenses for the first four years that a student attends an approved post-secondary institution.

- Lifetime Learning Credit. Parents can lower their tax bills by claiming the amount spent on tuition and receiving a 20% tax credit on the first $10,000 of qualified education expenses, to save as much as $2,000.2 Qualifying tuition includes undergraduate, graduate, or professional degree courses. In the 2020 tax year, the income for couples filing jointly must not exceed $138,000 to take advantage of this credit.

As a couple who files joint tax returns, you can also take deductions for your contributions to a traditional individual retirement account (IRA) and any expenses related to the adoption of a qualifying child.

Benefits of Married Filing Separately

Tax bills aside, there is one scenario in which married filing separately may be especially wise. If you do not want to be liable for your spouse's taxes and suspect that they are hiding income or claiming deductions or credits falsely, then filing separately is the best option.

Signing a joint return means that both spouses are responsible for the accuracy of the return and for any tax liabilities or penalties that may apply. By signing your own return and not a joint one, you are only responsible for the accuracy of your own information and for any tax liability and penalties that may ensue.

Special Considerations

If you live in community property states—Arizona, California, Idaho, Louisiana, Nevada, New Mexico, Texas, Washington, and Wisconsin—then you may need to see a tax professional, because the rules about separate incomes can be tricky.

Single Filer

What Is a Single Filer?

Single filers are taxpayers who file their federal income tax return with the IRS under the status "single." This filing status is used by a taxpayer who is unmarried and does not qualify for any other filing status.

Key Takeaways

- Single filer status is for people who are unmarried and do not qualify for any other filing status.

- Even if you are still married, you are considered unmarried by the IRS if you did not live with your spouse for the last six months of the tax year.

- Single people who can claim qualifying widow(er) or head of household status will find it advantageous to file under that status rather than as a single filer.

Understanding Single Filer

All persons who are required to file a federal income tax return with the IRS must choose a filing status. An individual can file under the following five statuses: single, married filing jointly, married filing separately, head of household, or qualifying widow(er) with dependent child. Tax rates

12

and standard deductions differ among the various filing statuses.

Single filers include people who on the last day of the year are unmarried or are legally separated from a spouse under a divorce or separate maintenance decree and do not qualify for another filing status. And though you may still be married, you are also considered unmarried by the IRS if you did not live with your spouse for the last six months of the tax year.

There are people who qualify to file single but may be better off claiming another filing status. If you meet the conditions for qualifying widow(er) or head of household, you will find that filing under either of those statuses will result in a lower tax bill.

If you qualify for more than one filing status, you are allowed to choose the one that results in the lowest tax bill.

Single Filer vs. Head of Household

Though many single people live alone and would consider themselves to be the head of their own household, the IRS distinguishes between a single filer and a person considered the head of a household. Head of household status only applies to unmarried persons who, for the given tax year, have paid more than half of the cost of maintaining a home for themselves and a qualifying person, such as a dependent.

According to the IRS, the costs of maintaining a home may include rent or mortgage payments, utility costs, repairs, property taxes, and food eaten at home.

$12,400

The amount of the standard deduction single filers can claim for 2020, which rises to $12,550 for the 2021 tax year. Heads of households qualify for a standard deduction of $18,650 in 2020 ($18,800 in 2021).

The qualifying person with whom a head of household lives must be their child, parent, or another type of relative. The person may be a domestic partner if that partner does not earn any income, which would qualify them as a dependent.

People who file as head of household pay a lower tax rate than people filing as single. They also must reach a higher income level before being obligated to pay income tax.6

Single Withholding vs. Married Withholding: What's the Difference?

In most cases, married couples who file taxes jointly have less withheld

When you start a new job, you will usually be asked to fill out a W-4 Form, or Employee's Withholding Certificate. Using the information you supply, your employer will calculate how much money to withhold from your paychecks to cover your federal income taxes when they come due.1 The first section of the W-4 asks you to check a box to indicate whether you are "Single or Married filing separately," "Married filing jointly or Qualifying widow(er)," or "Head of Household." This article explains what it means to check the boxes for single or married tax withholding.

Key Takeaways

- IRS Form W-4, which you file with your employer when you start a job, is used to calculate how much money will be withheld from your paycheck to cover taxes.

- The form asks whether you are single or married, as well as the number of your dependents, if any.

- In general, married couples who file their taxes jointly will have less withheld from their paychecks than singles.

Single Withholding vs. Married Withholding

The three boxes on the W-4 Form (Single or Married filing separately, Married filing jointly or Qualifying widow(er), and Head of Household) correspond to the filing statuses that taxpayers must choose from when they file their annual Form 1040 tax returns. (Form 1040 breaks them into five categories, giving "Single" and "Married filing separately," for example, their own check boxes.)

To qualify as a head of household (HOH), the taxpayer must be unmarried and supporting another person.

Married taxpayers can choose to file jointly on the same tax return, or separately on different tax returns, whichever is more advantageous in their situation. In most cases, filing a joint tax return will result in a lower tax bill.

Which box you check on your W-4 will determine the standard deduction and tax rates that are used to compute your withholding. Married taxpayers who plan to file jointly will have less withheld on a percentage basis than singles or people with other statuses. That is because married taxpayers are likely to pay less tax when they file their returns for the year.

The standard deduction for single taxpayers and married individuals filing separately, for example, is $12,400 for tax year 2020, while marrieds filing jointly get twice that, or $24,800. Similarly, singles are taxed at the lowest marginal tax rate of 10% on just their first $9,875 in income, while married couples filing jointly are taxed at that rate on their first $19,750 in income (again, for tax year 2020). At higher marginal tax brackets, married taxpayers continue to benefit. 4

If your marital status changes, you will want to submit a new W-4 Form so your employer can adjust your tax withholding.

How Dependents Fit In

The Internal Revenue Service (IRS) redesigned the W-4 form for 2020, a change necessitated by the Tax Cuts and Jobs Act's elimination of the personal exemption. So, if you have not filled out a W-4 in a few years, you will find it looks quite different today.

In particular, the form no longer asks you to calculate (or guess at) your number of withholding allowances. Instead, taxpayers whose income is under $400,000 (for marrieds filing jointly) or $200,000 (for other filing statuses) are instructed to multiply their number of qualifying children under age 17 by $2,000 and any other dependents by $500 and enter those dollar figures on the form.3

Using that information, plus your filing status, your employer will calculate how much to withhold from your pay.

Other Considerations

Bear in mind that if you have more money than necessary withheld from your paycheck you have lost the use of that money throughout the year, although you should get it back later as a tax refund. If you have too little withheld, you may face a big tax bill and an underpayment penalty.

Also note that you can always file a new W-4 with your employer to adjust your withholding. You will want to do that if your filing status changes from "single" to "married," or vice versa.

Active Income

What Is Active Income?

Active income refers to income received for performing a service. Wages, tips, salaries, commissions, and income from businesses in which there is material participation are examples of active income.

Key Takeaways

- The most common types of income are active, passive, and portfolio.

- Active income includes salaries, wages, commissions, and tips.

- For income from a business to be considered active rather than passive, the owner must satisfy the requirements for material participation, based on hours worked or other factors.

Understanding Active Income

There are three main categories of income: active income, passive (or unearned) income, and portfolio income.

Income received in the form of a paycheck from an employer is the most common example of active income.

For the self-employed or anyone else with an ownership interest in a business, income from business activities is considered active if it meets the Internal Revenue Service (IRS) definition of material participation. That means at least one of the following is true:

- The taxpayer works 500 or more hours in the business during the year.

- The taxpayer does most of the work in the business.

- The taxpayer works more than 100 hours in the business during the year, and no other staff works more hours than the taxpayer.2

If someone receives income from a business in which they do not actively participate, then that is considered passive income.

Portfolio income, meanwhile, is income from investments, such as dividends and capital gains.

These diverse types of income can be taxed differently, depending on the law at the time. For example, portfolio income is currently taxed at lower rates than active income.

Example of Active Income From a Business

Patrick and Emily, who are not married to each other, each have a 50% interest in an online business. Patrick does most of the day-to-day work in the business. Therefore, the IRS considers his income active. Emily assists with the marketing activities but works fewer than 100 hours a year in the business. Therefore, the IRS considers her income from the business to be passive.

The material participation rule was established to stop individuals who do not actively participate in a business from using it to generate tax losses that they could write off against their active income.

Business Income

What Is Business Income?

Business income is a type of earned income and is classified as ordinary income for tax purposes. It encompasses any income realized because of an entity's operations. In its simplest form, it is a business entity's net profit or loss, which is calculated as its revenue from all sources minus the costs of doing business.

Key Takeaways

- Business income is earned income and encompasses any income realized from an entity's operations.

- For tax purposes, business income is treated as ordinary income.

- Business expenses and losses often offset business income.

- How a business is taxed depends on whether it is a sole proprietorship, a partnership, or a corporation.

Understanding Business Income

Business income is a term commonly used in tax reporting. According to the Internal Revenue Service (IRS), "Business income may include income received from the sale of products or services. For example, fees received by a person from the regular practice of a profession are business income. Rents received by a person in the real estate business are business income. A business must include in income payments received in the form of property or services at the fair market value of the property or services."

Business expenses and business losses can offset business income, which can be either positive or negative in any given year. The profit motive behind business income is universal to most business entities. However, the way in which business income is taxed differs for each of the most common types of businesses: sole proprietorships, partnerships, and corporations.

How business income is taxed

How a business is formed determines how it should report its income to the IRS.

- A sole proprietorship is not a legally separate entity from its owner. Therefore, business income from a sole proprietorship is reported on that individual's Form 1040 tax return using Schedule C: Profit or Loss From Business.

- A partnership is an unincorporated business that is jointly owned by two or more individuals. It reports business income on Form 1065. However, the partnership itself does not pay income tax. All partners receive a Schedule K-1 and report their share of the partnership's income on their own individual income tax returns.

- A limited liability company (LLC) is like a hybrid between a corporation and a sole proprietorship or partnership. Single-member LLCs report business income on Form 1040, Schedule C. LLCs with more than one member use the same form used by partnerships: Form 1065. An LLC also can opt to be taxed as a C corporation (C-Corp) or an S corporation (S-Corp).

- A corporation is a legally separate entity from any individual who owns it. Corporations are each taxed as a C corporation (C-Corp), which means they are taxed separately from their owners. Business income from a corporation is reported on Form 1120.

- An S corporation (S-Corp) is a corporation that elects to be taxed as a pass-through business. Business income for an S-Corp is reported on Form 1120-S. Like a partnership, the S-Corp does not pay income tax. Shareholders receive a K-1 and report their share of the company's income on their individual tax returns. Note that an S-Corp is not a type of business entity; it is a tax filing election that an LLC or a C-Corp can elect after forming.

Business income coverage is a type of insurance that covers company losses due to a slowdown or temporary suspension of normal operations resulting from damage to a business's physical property.

Insurance Coverage for Business Income

A business income coverage form is a type of property insurance policy that covers a company's loss of income due to a slowdown or a temporary suspension of normal operations stemming from damage to its physical property. Let us say a doctor's office in Florida is damaged by a hurricane. The doctor is unable to see patients in that office until the building is structurally sound again. The business income coverage would kick in during the time when the doctor's business is interrupted.

Earned Income

What Is Earned Income?

Earned income includes money made from employment including wages, salaries, bonuses, commissions, tips, and net earnings from self-employment, according to the Internal Revenue Service (IRS) definition. It can also include long-term disability and union strike benefits and, in some cases, payments from certain deferred retirement compensation arrangements.

Earned income can be contrasted with unearned income, also known as a passive income, which is money not acquired through working.

Key Takeaways

- Earned income is any income that is received from a job or self-employment.

- Earned income may include wages, salary, tips, bonuses, and commissions.

- Income instead derived from investments and government benefit programs would not be considered earned income.

- Earned income is often taxed differently from unearned income.

- Employed taxpayers with lower incomes may be eligible for an earned income tax credit (EITC).

Understanding Earned Income

For tax purposes, earned income is any income you receive for work you have done, either for an employer or a business of your own.

Examples of income that is not considered "earned" include government benefits, such as payments from the Temporary Assistance for Needy Families program (often referred to as welfare), unemployment, workers' compensation, and Social Security. Also in this category are disbursements from non-deferred pensions and retirement plans, alimony, capital gains, interest income from a bank account, stock dividends, bond interest, and passive income generated from rental property.

Both earned income and other types of income are taxable, although sometimes at different percentage rates. For tax year 2020, for example, the federal government taxes earned income at seven separate rates (or brackets), ranging from 10% on the first $19,750 ($19,900 in 2021) in income for married couples filing jointly to 37% for any income over $622,050 ($628,300 in 2021), again for married couples filing jointly. The thresholds are different for singles, married couples who file separately, and heads of households.

However, long-term capital gains on assets held for a year or more (which are classified as portfolio income) are taxed at 0%, 15%, and 20%, depending on the amount and the taxpayer's filing status. Short-term capital gains, which cover assets held for less than a year, are taxed at the same rate as a taxpayer's earned income.

Having earned income can affect whether a retiree's Social Security benefits are taxable.

Special Considerations

Determining whether income is earned or unearned—and reporting it on the appropriate lines of a Form 1040 or other tax return—is a straightforward process. For some taxpayers, however, earned income can have ramifications that are worth taking into consideration.

If you are receiving Social Security benefits, for example, you may have to pay income tax on a portion of those benefits if you have earned income (or other income) over a certain threshold. In that case, either 50% or 85% of your benefits will be subject to tax, depending on your income and filing status.6 This can be an important consideration for people who plan to continue working after they are eligible for Social Security benefits or are deciding whether to delay filing for benefits.

If you are self-employed, you also need to consider how much earned (and other) income you expect to have for the year and pay estimated taxes each quarter based on that amount. If you fail to pay enough tax throughout the year, you will have to make it up when you file your tax return and you may also be subject to IRS penalties.

The Earned Income Tax Credit (EITC)

If you have a low earned income—and meet other qualifications—you may be eligible for the federal earned income tax credit (EIC or EITC), which can reduce your tax bill or result in a refund.

To qualify for the credit, you must file a tax return even if you do not owe any tax or would not otherwise be required to file one.

The EITC was conceived of as a type of "work bonus plan" to supplement the wages of low-income workers, help offset the effect of Social Security taxes, and encourage work to move people off welfare. It continues to be viewed as an anti-poverty tax benefit aimed to reward people for employment.

Note that as part of the American Rescue Plan Act of 2021, the EITC cap is temporarily raised from $543 for childless households to $1,502 for 2021. The bill also expands eligibility for childless households.9 Also, since many taxpayers' 2020 incomes were lower than their 2019 incomes due to the COVID-19 pandemic, the EITC claimed on 2020 tax returns could be based on either 2019 or 2020 earnings.

As usual in these matters, if you are unsure about whether you qualify or have questions about your specific situation, you should seek advice from the IRS or an independent tax expert.

Earned Income FAQs

What Are Some Common Examples of Earned Income?

According to the IRS, earned income only includes money received as pay for work performed. Earned income includes only wages/salary, commissions, bonuses, and business income (minus expenses if the person is self-employed).

What Are Some Examples of Unearned Income?

Examples of unearned income include interest from savings, CDs, or other bank accounts, bond interest, alimony, capital gains, and dividends from stock. Income from retirement accounts, inheritances, gifts, welfare payments, rental income, lottery or gambling winnings, and annuities are all also classified as unearned income.

What Is the Difference Between Earned and Unearned Income?

Aside from the differences in how the income is generated (i.e., earned through working or not), the IRS may treat each differently for tax purposes. Tax rates vary among sources of unearned income, with most unearned income sources not subject to payroll taxes, and none of it is subject to employment taxes such as Social Security and Medicare. Additionally, unearned income cannot be used for making contributions to a qualified retirement account such as an IRA.

Gross Income

What Is Gross Income?

Gross income for an individual—also known as gross pay when it is on a paycheck—is the individual's total pay from their employer before taxes or other deductions. This includes income from all sources and is not limited to income received in cash; it also includes property or services received. Gross annual income is the amount of money that a person earns in one year before taxes and includes income from all sources.

For companies, gross income is interchangeable with gross margin or gross profit. A company's gross income, found on the income statement, is the revenue from all sources minus the firm's cost of goods sold (COGS).

Gross Income

Key Takeaways

- Gross income for an individual consists of income from wages and salary plus other forms of income, including pensions, interest, dividends, and rental income.

- Gross income for a business, also known as gross profit or gross margin, includes the gross revenue of the firm less cost of goods sold, but it does not include all the other costs involved in running the business.

- Individual gross income is part of an income tax return and—after certain deductions and exemptions—becomes adjusted gross income, then taxable income.

Understanding Gross Income

Individual Gross Income

An individual's gross income is used by lenders or property owners to determine whether said individual is a worthy borrower or renter. When filing federal and state income taxes, gross income is the starting point before subtracting deductions to determine the amount of tax owed.

For individuals, the gross income metric used on the income tax return includes not just wages or salary but also other forms of income, such as tips, capital gains, rental payments, dividends, alimony, pension, and interest. After subtracting above-the-line tax deductions, the result is adjusted gross income (AGI).

Continuing down the tax form, below-the-line deductions are taken from AGI and result in a taxable income figure. After applying any allowed deductions or exemptions, the resulting taxable income can be significantly less than an individual's gross income.

There are income sources that are not included in gross income for tax purposes but still may be included when calculating gross income for a lender or creditor. Common nontaxable income sources are certain Social Security benefits, life insurance payouts, some inheritances or gifts, and state or municipal bond interest.

Business Gross Income

A company's gross income, or gross profit margin, is the simplest measure of the firm's profitability. While the gross income metric includes the direct cost of producing or providing goods and services, it does not include other costs related to selling activities, administration, taxes, and other costs related to running the overall business.

Example of Individual Gross Income

Assume that an individual has a $75,000 annual salary, generates $1,000 a year in interest from a savings account, collects $500 per year in stock dividends, and receives $10,000 a year from rental property income. Their gross annual income is $86,500.

Example of Business Gross Income

Gross income is a line item that is sometimes included in a company's income statement but is not required. If not displayed, it is calculated as gross revenue minus COGS.

Gross Income=Gross Revenue−COGS COGS=Cost of Goods Sold {Gross Income} = {Gross Revenue} - {COGS} {COGS} = \Cost of Goods Sold}Gross Income=Gross Revenue−COGS COGS=Cost of Goods Sold

Gross income is sometimes referred to as gross margin. Then there's gross profit margin, which is more correctly defined as a percentage and is used as a profitability metric. The gross income for a company reveals how much money it has made on its products or services after subtracting the direct costs to make the product or provide the service.

Adjusted Gross Income (AGI)

What Is Adjusted Gross Income (AGI)?

Adjusted gross income (AGI) is a figure that the Internal Revenue Service uses to determine your income tax liability for the year. It is calculated by subtracting certain adjustments from gross income, such as business expenses, student loan interest payments, and other expenses.1

After calculating AGI, the next step is to subtract deductions to determine the taxpayers' taxable income. In addition, the IRS also uses other income metrics, such as modified AGI (MAGI) for certain programs and retirement accounts.

Key Takeaways

- The Internal Revenue Service uses your adjusted gross income (AGI) to determine how much income tax you owe for the year.

- AGI is calculated by taking all your income for the year (your gross income) and subtracting certain "adjustments to income."

- Your AGI can affect the size of your tax deductions as well as your eligibility for some types of retirement plan contributions.

- Modified adjusted gross income is your AGI with some otherwise-allowable deductions added back in. For many people, AGI and MAGI will be the same.

Understanding Adjusted Gross Income (AGI)

As prescribed in the United States tax code, adjusted gross income is a modification of gross income. Gross income is simply the sum of all the money you earned in a year, which may include wages, dividends, capital gains, interest income, royalties, rental income, alimony, and retirement distributions. AGI makes certain adjustments to your gross income to reach the figure on which your tax liability will be calculated.

Many states in the U.S. also use the AGI from federal returns to calculate how much individuals owe in state income taxes. States may modify this number further with state-specific deductions and credits.

The items subtracted from your gross income to calculate your AGI are referred to as adjustments to income, and you report them on Schedule 1 of your tax return when you file your annual tax return. Some of the most common adjustments are listed here, along with the separate tax forms on which a few of them are calculated:

- Alimony payments

- Early withdrawal penalties on savings

- Educator expenses

- Employee business expenses for armed forces reservists, qualified performing artists, fee-basis state or local government officials, and employees with impairment-related work expenses (Form 2106)

- Health savings account (HSA) deductions (Form 8889)

- Moving expenses for members of the armed forces (Form 3903)

- Self-employed SEP, SIMPLE, and qualified plans

- Self-employed health insurance deduction

- Self-employment tax (the deductible portion)

- Student loan interest deduction

- Tuition and fees (Form 8917)

Calculating Your Adjusted Gross Income (AGI)

If you use software to prepare your tax return, it will calculate your AGI once you input your numbers. If you calculate it yourself, you will begin by tallying your reported income for the year. That might include job income, as reported to the IRS by your employer on a W-2 form, plus any income, such as dividends and miscellaneous income, reported on 1099 forms.

Next, you add any taxable income from other sources, such as profit on the sale of a property, unemployment compensation, pensions, Social Security payments, or anything else that has not already been reported to the IRS. Many of these income items are also listed on IRS Schedule 1.

The next step is to subtract the applicable adjustments to income listed above from your reported income. The resulting figure is your adjusted gross income.

To determine your taxable income, subtract either the standard deduction or your total itemized deductions from your AGI. In most cases, you can choose whichever gives you the most benefit. For example, the standard deduction for 2020 tax returns for married couples filing jointly is $24,800 ($25,100 for 2021), so couples whose itemized deductions exceed that amount would opt to itemize, while others would simply take the standard deduction.

The IRS provides a list of itemized deductions and the requirements for claiming them on its website.

Your AGI also affects your eligibility for many of the deductions and credits available on your tax return. In general, the lower your AGI, the greater the amount of deductions and credits you will be eligible to claim, and the more you will be able to reduce your tax bill.

An Example of Adjusted Gross Income (AGI) Affecting Deductions

Let us say you had some significant dental expenses during the year that were not reimbursed by insurance, and you have decided to itemize your deductions. You are allowed to deduct the portion of those expenses that exceed 7.5% of your AGI.

This means if you report $12,000 in unreimbursed dental expenses and have an AGI of $100,000, you can deduct the amount that exceeds $7,500, which is $4,500. However, if your AGI is $50,000, the 7.5% reduction is just $3,750, and you would be entitled to an $8,250 deduction.

Adjusted Gross Income (AGI) vs. Modified Adjusted Gross Income (MAGI)

In addition to AGI, some tax calculations and government programs call for using what is known as your modified adjusted gross income, or MAGI. This figure starts with your adjusted gross income then adds back certain items, such as any deductions you take for student loan interest or tuition and fees.

Your MAGI is used to determine how much, if anything, you can contribute to a Roth IRA in any given year. It is also used to calculate your income if you apply for Marketplace health insurance under the Affordable Care Act (ACA).

Many people with uncomplicated financial lives find that their AGI and MAGI are the same number, or close.

If you file your taxes electronically, the IRS form will ask you for your previous year's AGI as a way of verifying your identity.

Special Considerations

You report your AGI on line 8b of IRS Form 1040 that you use to file your income taxes for the year. Keep that number handy after completing your taxes because you will need it again if you e-file your taxes next year. The IRS uses it to verify your identity.

Also note that if your AGI is under a certain amount ($72,000 in 2020), you are eligible to use the IRS Free File program to file your federal (and in some cases, state) taxes electronically at no charge.

What Does Adjusted Gross Income (AGI) Mean for Tax Payments?

AGI is your income for the year after accounting for all applicable tax deductions. It is an important number that is used by the IRS to determine how much you owe in taxes. AGI is calculated by taking your gross income from the year and subtracting any deductions that you are eligible to claim. Therefore, your AGI will always be less than or equal to your gross income.

What Are Some Common Adjustments Used When Determining AGI?

There are a wide variety of adjustments that might be made when calculating AGI, depending on the financial and life circumstances of the filer. Moreover, since the tax laws can be changed by lawmakers, the list of available adjustments can change over time. Some of the most common adjustments used when calculating AGI include reductions for alimony, student loan interest payments, and tuition costs for qualifying institutions.

What Is the Difference Between AGI and Modified Adjusted Gross Income (MAGI)?

AGI and MAGI are remarkably similar, except that MAGI adds back certain deductions. For this reason, MAGI would always be larger than or equal to AGI. Common examples of deductions that are added back to calculate MAGI include foreign earned income, income earned on U.S. savings bonds, and losses arising from a publicly traded partnership.

Modified Adjusted Gross Income (MAGI)

What Is Modified Adjusted Gross Income (MAGI)?

Your modified adjusted gross income (MAGI) is your adjusted gross income (AGI) after considering certain allowable deductions and any tax penalties. For many taxpayers, the numbers are the same.

In any case, your modified adjusted gross income (MAGI) is an important number to understand since it can help with the following:

- Reduce your taxable income to account for your retirement account contributions.

- Factor in your eligibility for benefits like the student loan interest deduction and the child tax credit.

- Establish your eligibility for income-based Medicaid coverage or a health insurance subsidy.

Key Takeaways

- Modified adjusted gross income, or MAGI, adjusts the AGI for certain tax deductions and credits.

- You will have to crunch some numbers to find your MAGI, but tax prep software makes this work easy.

- MAGI can change your eligibility for certain programs like qualified retirement account contributions.

Modified Adjusted Gross Income (MAGI)

Understanding Modified Adjusted Gross Income

MAGI can be defined as your household's adjusted gross income after any tax-exempt interest income, and certain deductions are factored in.

The Internal Revenue Service (IRS) uses MAGI to establish whether you qualify for certain tax benefits. Most notably, MAGI determine:

- Whether your income does not exceed the level that qualifies you to contribute to a Roth IRA.

- Whether you can deduct your traditional individual retirement account (IRA) contributions if you and/or your spouse have retirement plans, such as a 401(k) at work.

- Whether you are eligible for the premium tax credit which lowers your health insurance costs if you buy a plan through a state or federal Health Insurance Marketplace.

For example, you can contribute to a traditional IRA no matter how much money you earn. Typically, you can deduct the IRA contribution amount, reducing your taxable income for that tax year. However, you cannot deduct those contributions when you file your tax return if your MAGI exceed limits set by the IRS and you and/or your spouse have a retirement plan at work.

How Modified Adjusted Gross Income Works

Determining your MAGI is a three-step process:

1. Figure out your gross income for the year

2. Calculate your adjusted gross income (AGI)

3. Add back certain deductions to calculate your MAGI2

Figure out your gross income

Your gross income includes everything you earned during the year from:

- Alimony, which are court-ordered payments to a spouse due to divorce or separation7

- Business income

- Capital gains or any realized gains after selling an asset for a profit

- Dividends, which are typically cash payments to a company's shareholders

- Interest

- Farm income

- Rental and royalty income

- Retirement income

- Tips

- Wages

There are two scenarios in which alimony payments are not considered gross income. The first is if your divorce agreement was executed after 2018. The second is if your divorce agreement was executed before 2019 but later modified to expressly state that such payments are not deductible for the payer.

Your gross income appears on line 9 of Form 1040.

Calculate your AGI (or find it on your tax return)

Your adjusted gross income (AGI) is important because it is the total taxable income calculated before itemized or standard deductions, exemptions, and credits are considered. It dictates how you can use various tax credits and exemptions. For example, AGI affects the amount of money you can claim for the child tax credit.

Your adjusted gross income is equal to your gross income, minus certain tax-deductible expenses, including:

- Certain business expenses for performing artists, reservists, and fee-basis government officials

- Educator expenses

- Half of any self-employment taxes

- Health insurance premiums (if you are self-employed)

- Health savings account (HSA) contributions

- Moving expenses for members of the armed forces moving due to active duty

- Penalties on early withdrawal of savings

- Retirement plan contributions (including IRAs and self-employed retirement plan contributions)

- Student loan interest

- Tuition and fees

You can do the math to figure out your AGI, or you can find it on line 11 of Form 1040.9

Add back certain deductions

To find your MAGI, take your AGI and add back:

- Any deductions you took for IRA contributions and taxable Social Security payments

- Excluded foreign income

- Interest from EE savings bonds used to pay for higher education expenses

- Losses from a partnership

- Passive income or loss

- Rental losses

- The exclusion for adoption expenses

Many of these deductions are not commonly used, so your MAGI and AGI could be similar or even identical.

Special Considerations for MAGI

Roth IRAs

To contribute to a Roth IRA, your MAGI must be below the limits specified by the IRS. If you are within the income threshold, the actual amount you can contribute is also determined by your MAGI. If your MAGI exceed the allowed limits, your contributions are phased out.

Here are the Roth IRA income limits for 2021:

2021 Roth IRA Income Limits		
If your filing status is...	And your modified AGI is...	You can contribute...
Married filing jointly or qualifying widow(er)	Less than $198,000	Up to the limit
	More than $198,000 but less than $208,000	A reduced amount
	$208,000 or more	Zero
Single, head of household, or married filing separately and you did not live with your spouse at any time during the year	Less than $125,000	Up to the limit
	More than $125,000 but less than $140,000	A reduced amount
	$140,000 or more	Zero
Married filing separately and you lived with your spouse at any time during the year	Less than $10,000	A reduced amount
	$10,000 or more	Zero

Here is a rundown of Roth IRA income limits for 2020:

2020 Roth IRA Income Limits		
If your filing status is…	And your modified AGI is…	You can contribute…
Married filing jointly or qualifying widow(er)	Less than $196,000	Up to the limit
	More than $196,000 but less than $206,000	A reduced amount
	$206,000 or more	Zero
Single, head of household, or married filing separately and you did not live with your spouse at any time during the year	Less than $124,000	Up to the limit
	More than $124,000 but less than $139,000	A reduced amount
	$139,000 or more	Zero
Married filing separately and you lived with your spouse at any time during the year	Less than $10,000	A reduced amount
	$10,000 or more	Zero

Note that if you contribute more than you are allowed, you must remove the excess contributions. Otherwise, you will face a tax penalty. Excess contributions are taxed at a rate of 6% per year for as long as the excess amount remains in your IRA.

Traditional IRAs

Your MAGI and whether you and your spouse have retirement plans at work determine whether you can deduct traditional IRA contributions. If neither spouse is covered by a plan at work, you can take the full deduction up to the amount of your contribution limit. However, if either spouse has a plan at work, your deduction could be limited.

Here is a rundown of traditional IRA income limits for 2021.

2021 Traditional IRA Income Limits		
If your filing status is…	And your modified AGI is…	Then you can take…
Single, head of household, qualifying widow(er), married filing jointly or separately and neither spouse is covered by a plan at work	Any amount	A full deduction up to the amount of your contribution limit
Married filing jointly or qualifying widow(er) and you are covered by a plan at work	$105,000 or less	A full deduction up to the amount of your contribution limit

2021 Traditional IRA Income Limits		
If your filing status is…	And your modified AGI is…	Then you can take…
	More than $105,000 but less than $125,000	A partial deduction
	$125,000 or more	No deduction
Married filing jointly and your spouse is covered by a plan at work	$198,000 or less	A full deduction up to the amount of your contribution limit
	More than $198,000 but less than $208,000	A partial deduction
	$208,000 or more	No deduction
Single or head of household and you are covered by a plan at work	$66,000 or less	A full deduction up to the amount of your contribution limit
	More than $66,000 but less than $76,000	A partial deduction
	$76,000 or more	No deduction
Married filing separately and either spouse is covered by a plan at work	Less than $10,000	A partial deduction
	$10,000 or more	No deduction

Here is a rundown of traditional IRA income limits for 2020.

2020 Traditional IRA Income Limits		
If your filing status is…	And your modified AGI is…	Then you can take…
Single, head of household, qualifying widow(er), married filing jointly or separately and neither spouse is covered by a plan at work	Any amount	A full deduction up to the amount of your contribution limit
Married filing jointly or qualifying widow(er) and you are covered by a plan at work	$104,000 or less	A full deduction up to the amount of your contribution limit
	More than $104,000 but less than $124,000	A partial deduction
	$124,000 or more	No deduction
Married filing jointly and your spouse is covered by a plan at work	$196,000 or less	A full deduction up to the amount of your contribution limit

2020 Traditional IRA Income Limits		
If your filing status is...	And your modified AGI is...	Then you can take...
	More than $196,000 but less than $206,000	A partial deduction
	$206,000 or more	No deduction
Single or head of household and you are covered by a plan at work	$65,000 or less	A full deduction up to the amount of your contribution limit
	More than $65,000 but less than $75,000	A partial deduction
	$75,000 or more	No deduction
Married filing separately and either spouse is covered by a plan at work	Less than $10,000	A partial deduction
	$10,000 or more	No deduction

Tax laws are complicated and do change periodically. If you need help figuring out your MAGI, or if you have any questions about IRA contribution and income limits, contact a trusted tax professional.

How Do I Calculate My Modified Adjusted Gross Income (MAGI)?

Calculating your MAGI is straightforward. To do so, first, calculate your adjusted gross income (AGI) and then add back any of the deductions specified by the IRS that apply to your situation. Examples of these deductions include income from foreign sources, interest from certain savings bonds, and expenses related to adopting a child. Because MAGI involve adding back these deductions, MAGI will always be greater than or equal to AGI. To calculate your modified adjusted gross income (MAGI):

- Add up your gross income from all sources.

- Check the list of "adjustments" to your gross income and add those that you qualify for to your gross income. The list is on the 1040 form.

- The resulting number is your adjusted gross income (AGI).

- Add back any deductions you qualify for, which can include student loan interest and IRA contributions.

- The resulting number is your MAGI. It is not unusual for it to be the same as your AGI.

What Purpose does MAGI Serve?

The IRS uses MAGI to determine whether you qualify for certain tax programs and benefits. For instance, it helps determine the size of your Roth IRA contributions. Knowing your MAGI can also help avoid facing tax penalties because over-contributing to these programs and others like them can trigger interest payments and fines. Your MAGI can also determine eligibility for certain government programs, such as the subsidized insurance plans available on the Health Insurance Marketplace.

Can MAGI and AGI be the Same?

Yes, MAGI and AGI can be the same. For many people, the list of deductions that need to be added back to AGI to calculate MAGI will not be relevant. For instance, those who did not earn any foreign income would have no reason to use that deduction and would not add back those earnings to their AGI. For them, AGI and MAGI would therefore be the same number.

Ordinary Income

What Is Ordinary Income?

Ordinary income is any type of income earned by an organization or an individual that is taxable at ordinary rates. It includes (but is not limited to) wages, salaries, tips, bonuses, rents, royalties, and interest income from bonds and commissions.

Key Takeaways

- Ordinary income is any type of income that is taxable at ordinary rates.

- Examples of ordinary income include wages, salaries, tips, bonuses, rents, royalties, and interest income from bonds and commissions.

- For individuals, ordinary income usually consists of the pretax salaries and wages that they have earned.

- In a corporate setting, ordinary income comes from regular day-to-day business operations, excluding income gained from selling capital assets.

Understanding Ordinary Income

Ordinary income comes in two forms: personal income, and business income. From a personal perspective, ordinary income can be defined as any kind of cash inflow that is subject to income tax, as outlined by the Internal Revenue Service (IRS).

In a corporate setting, the term refers to any type of income generated from regular day-to-day business operations, excluding any income earned from the sale of long-term capital assets, such as land or equipment.

Long-term capital gains—the increase in the value of investments owned for more than a year—and qualified dividends are taxed differently and not considered to be ordinary income.

Examples of Ordinary Income

Let us look at how ordinary income works for individuals and businesses in the following examples.

Individuals

For private individuals, ordinary income typically consists of the salaries and wages that they earn from their employers before tax. If, for example, a person holds a customer service job at Target and earns $3,000 per month, then their annual ordinary income can be calculated by multiplying $3,000 by 12.

If this customer service employee has no other income sources, then $36,000 is the amount that would be taxed on their year-end tax return as gross income. Alternatively, if the same person also owned property and earned $1,000 a month in rental income, then their ordinary income would increase to $48,000 per year.

Businesses

For businesses, ordinary income is the pretax profit earned from selling its product(s) or service(s). Retailer Target made $78.1 billion in total revenue in the year ending Feb. 1, 2020, its most recent fiscal year (FY).

However, those sales cost money to generate. The company claimed that the costs attributable to the production of goods sold (COGS) were $54.8 billion. Target also said it forked out $16.2 billion on selling, general, and administrative expenses (SG&As). Factor in depreciation and amortization, as well as the loss of value of its tangible and intangible assets, and you get an ordinary income of $4.6 billion. This is the amount of income that Target was taxed on.

Ordinary income can only be offset with standard tax deductions, while capital gains can only be offset with capital losses.

Special Considerations

To encourage people to invest in the long term, the government taxes capital gains and common stock dividends at a lower rate than ordinary income. Dividends were taxed as ordinary income—up to 38.6%—until the Jobs and Growth Tax Relief Reconciliation Act of 2003 (JGTRRA) was enacted, reducing the tax on most dividend income, along with some capital gains, to 15%. Those changes encouraged investing and prompted companies to increase dividends or begin paying dividends.

At the end of 2017, then-President Donald Trump signed the Tax Cuts and Jobs Act (TCJA) into law, which changed the tax rate on qualified dividends (see below) to 0%, 15%, or 20%, depending on an individual's taxable income and filing status.

Qualified vs. unqualified dividends

Investors should be aware that not all dividends qualify for favorable tax treatment. Examples of unqualified dividends include those paid out by real estate investment trusts (REITs) and master limited partnerships (MLPs), income paid on employee stock options (ESOs), and dividends paid by tax-exempt companies and on savings accounts or money market accounts.

Another thing to watch out for is eligibility requirements. Regular dividends paid out to shareholders of for-profit companies usually qualify for taxation at the reduced capital gains rate, but investors must adhere to minimum holding periods to take advantage.

For common stock, a share must be held for more than 60 days of the holding period, the 120-day period that begins 60 days before the ex-dividend date. For preferred stock, the holding period is longer, beginning 90 days before the company's ex-dividend date.

Passive Income

What Is Passive Income?

Passive income is earnings derived from a rental property, limited partnership, or other enterprise in which a person is not actively involved. As with active income, passive income is usually taxable, but it is often treated differently by the IRS.

Key Takeaways

- Passive income is earnings from a rental property, limited partnership, or other business in which a person is not actively involved.

- The IRS has specific rules for what it calls material participation, which determine whether a taxpayer has actively participated in business, rental, or other income-producing activity.

- A taxpayer can claim a passive loss against income generated from passive activities.

Passive Income

Understanding Passive Income

There are three main categories of income: active income, passive income, and portfolio income. Passive incomes include earnings from a rental property, limited partnership, or other business in which a person is not actively involved—a silent investor, for example.

Proponents of earning passive income tend to be boosters of a work-from-home and be-your-own-boss professional lifestyle. Passive income has been a loosely used term in recent years. Colloquially, it has been used to define money being earned regularly with little or no effort on the part of the person receiving it.

Passive income, when used as a technical term, is defined by the IRS as either "net rental income" or "income from a business in which the taxpayer does not materially participate," and in some cases can include self-charged interest.

Portfolio income is considered passive income by some analysts, so dividends and interest would be considered passive. However, the IRS does not always agree that portfolio income is passive, so it is wise to check with a tax professional on that subject.

Types of Passive Income

Types of passive income include self-charged interest, rental properties, and businesses in which the person receiving income does not materially participate. There are specific IRS rules that need to be followed for income to be considered passive.

Self-charged interest

When money is loaned to a partnership or an S corporation acting as a pass-through entity (a business that is designed to reduce the effects of double taxation) by that entity's owner, the interest income on that loan to the portfolio income can qualify as passive income. "Certain self-charged interest income or deductions may be treated as passive activity gross income or passive activity deductions if the loan proceeds are used in a passive activity," the IRS states.

Rental properties

Rental properties are defined as passive income with a couple of exceptions. If you are a real estate professional, any rental income you are making counts as active income. If you are "self-renting," meaning that you own a space and are renting it out to a corporation or partnership where you conduct business, that does not constitute passive income unless that lease had been signed before 1988, in which case you have been exempted into having that income defined as passive. The IRS notes, "It doesn't matter whether or not the use is under a lease, a service contract, or some other arrangement."

However, income from leasing land does not qualify as passive income. Despite this, a landowner can benefit from passive income loss rules if the property nets a loss during the tax year.3

If you hold land for investment, any earnings would be considered active.

'No material participation' in a business

If you put $500,000 into a candy store with the agreement that the owners would pay you a percentage of earnings, that would be considered passive income if you do not participate in the operation of the business in any meaningful way other than making the investment. If you helped manage the company with the owners, your income could be seen as active, because you provided "material participation."

The IRS has standards for material participation that include the following:

- If you have dedicated more than 500 hours to a business or activity from which you are profiting, that is material participation.

- If your participation in an activity has been "substantially all" of the participation for that tax year, that is material participation.

- If you have participated up to 100 hours and that is at least as much as any other person involved in the activity, that also is defined as material participation.

Special Considerations

When you record a loss on a passive activity, only passive activity profits can have their deductions offset as opposed to the income. It would be prudent to ensure that all your passive activities were classified that way, to make the most of the tax deduction. These deductions are allocated for the next tax year and are applied in a reasonable manner that considers the next year's earnings or losses.

To save time and effort, you can group two or more passive activities into one larger activity, provided you form an "appropriate economic unit," according to the IRS. When you do this, instead of having to provide material participation in multiple activities, you only must provide it for the activity. In addition, if you include multiple activities in one group and must dispose of one of those activities, you have only done away with part of a larger activity as opposed to all a smaller one.

The organizing principle behind this grouping is simple: if the activities are in the same geographic area; if the activities have similarities in the types of business; or if the activities are somehow interdependent—for instance, if they have the same customers, employees, or use a single set of books for accounting.

If, for example, you owned a pretzel store and a sneaker store located in malls in both Monterey, Calif., and Amarillo, Texas, you would have four options for how to group their passive income:

- Grouped into one activity (all businesses were in shopping malls)

- Grouped by geography (Monterey and Amarillo)

- Grouped by type of business (retail sales of pretzels and shoes)

- Or they could remain ungrouped

Personal Income

What Is Personal Income?

Personal income refers to all income collectively received by all individuals or households in a country. Personal income includes compensation from a number of sources, including salaries, wages, and bonuses received from employment or self-employment, dividends and distributions received from investments, rental receipts from real estate investments, and profit sharing from businesses.

Key Takeaways

- Personal income is the amount of money collectively received by the inhabitants of a country.

- Sources of personal income include money earned from employment, dividends and distributions paid by investments, rents derived from property ownership, and profit sharing from businesses.

- Personal income is subject to taxation.

Understanding Personal Income

The term personal income is sometimes used to refer to the total compensation received by an individual, but this is more aptly referred to as individual income. In most jurisdictions, personal income, also called gross income, is subject to taxation above a certain base amount.

Personal income has a significant effect on consumer consumption. As consumer spending drives much of the economy, national statistical organizations, economists, and analysts track personal income on a quarterly or annual basis. In the United States, the Bureau of Economic Analysis (BEA) tracks personal income statistics each month and compares them to numbers from the previous month. The agency also breaks out the numbers into categories, such as personal income earned through employment wages, rental income, farming, and sole proprietorships. This allows the agency to make analyses about how earning trends are changing.

Personal income tends to rise during periods of economic expansion and stagnate or decline slightly during recessionary times. Rapid economic growth since the 1980s in economies such as China, India, and Brazil have spurred substantial increases in personal incomes for millions of their citizens.

Personal Income vs. Disposable Personal Income

Disposable personal income (DPI) refers to the amount of money a population has left after taxes have been paid. It differs from personal income in that it takes taxes into account. However, it is important to note that contributions to government social insurance are not considered when calculating personal income.

Only income taxes are removed from the personal income figure when calculating disposable personal income.

Personal Income vs. Personal Consumption Expenditures

Personal income is often compared to personal consumption expenditures (PCE). PCE measures the changes in the price of consumer goods and services. By taking these changes into account, analysts can ascertain how changes in personal income affect spending. To illustrate, if personal income significantly increases one month, and PCE also increases, consumers collectively may have more cash in their pockets but may also have to spend more money on basic goods and services.

Taxable Income

What Is Taxable Income?

Taxable income is the portion of an individual's or a company's income used to calculate how much tax they owe the government in a given tax year. It can be described broadly as adjusted gross income (AGI) minus allowable itemized or standard deductions. Taxable income includes wages, salaries, bonuses, and tips, as well as investment income and several types of unearned income.

Key Takeaways

- Taxable income is the portion of a person's or company's gross income that the government deems subject to taxes.

- Taxable income consists of both earned and unearned income.

- Taxable income is less than adjusted gross income because of deductions that reduce it.

Taxable Income

Understanding Taxable Income

Unearned income considered to be taxable income includes canceled debts, alimony payments, child support, government benefits (such as unemployment benefits and disability payments), strike benefits, and lottery payments. Taxable income also includes earnings generated from appreciated assets that have been sold during the year and from dividends and interest income.

When it comes to deductions, the Internal Revenue Service (IRS) offers individual tax filers the option to claim the standard deduction or a list of itemized deductions. Itemized deductions include interest paid on mortgages, medical expenses exceeding a specific threshold (7.5% of AGI for 2020), and a range of other expenses.

When businesses file their taxes, they do not report their revenue directly as taxable income. Rather, they subtract their business expenses from their revenue to calculate their business income. Then, they subtract deductions to calculate their taxable income.

While canceled debts are usually taxable, Congress exempted forgiven Paycheck Protection Program (PPP) loans from federal taxation. Some states, however, may treat the forgiven amount as taxable income or disallow deductions for expenses paid for by the loan.

Calculating Taxable Income

Step 1: Determine Your Filing Status

To calculate your taxable income for an individual tax return, you first need to determine your filing status. If you are unmarried, you can file your taxes either as a single filer or, if you have a qualifying person for whom you pay more than half of the support and housing costs, as a head of household. If you are married, you will want to file as married filing jointly (MFJ). However, there are some limited instances where it may make sense to file as married filing separately (MFS).

Step 2: Gather Documents for All Sources of Income

Once you know your filing status, you will need to gather documents for all sources of income for yourself, your spouse (if applicable), and any dependents (if applicable). The total of all these sources of income is known as your gross income. Below are the most common tax forms that you will need to calculate your gross income.

- Form W-2 shows the income you earned through services performed as an employee.

- If you worked a contract job or side gig, then you will need a Form 1099-NEC (nonemployee compensation). It reports income earned while working for a non-employer person or entity (when those amounts are greater than $600).

- Form 1099-MISC reports amounts earned (greater than $600) from other income sources, including rents, prizes, fishing boat proceeds, or crop insurance payments.

- If you earned more than $10 in interest during the tax year, then you will receive a Form 1099-INT from your financial institution.

Step 3: Calculate Your Adjusted Gross Income

The next step is to calculate your adjusted gross income (AGI). Your AGI is the result of taking certain "above-the-line" adjustments to your gross income, such as contributions to a qualifying individual retirement account (IRA), student loan interest, and certain educator expenses. These items are referred to as "above the line" because they reduce your income before taking any allowable itemized deductions or standard deductions.

For the 2020 tax year, the CARES Act allows taxpayers who elect the standard deduction to take a $300 "above-the-line" deduction for cash contributions to charity.

Step 4: Calculate Your Deductions (Standard or Itemized)

The next step is to calculate your deductions. As mentioned above, you can either take the standard deduction or itemize your deductions.

The standard deduction is a set amount that tax filers can claim if they do not have enough itemized deductions to claim. For 2021, individual tax filers can claim a $12,400 standard deduction

($24,800 for married filing jointly and $18,650 for heads of household). These figures rise to $12,550, $25,100, and $18,800, respectively, for 2021.

If you plan to itemize deductions rather than take the standard deduction, these are the records most needed:

- Property taxes and mortgage interest paid. This typically appears on a Form 1098, Mortgage Interest Statement, which you will receive from your mortgage lender.1 If you have no mortgage or do not have an escrow account paying your property taxes, then you will need to keep a record of your property tax payments separately.

- State and local taxes paid. This is on the W-2 form if you work for an employer. If you are an independent contractor, then you will need a record of the estimated tax payments that you made quarterly throughout the year.

- Charitable donations. Charitable donations are a tax-deductible expense; however, the amount you can claim is limited to a percentage of your AGI in most years.

- Educational expenses. Be aware that if you pay qualifying educational expenses with a student loan, then it must be claimed in the year when the expenses are made, not in the year when the loan proceeds are received or repaid.

- Unreimbursed medical bills. For 2020, you can deduct the amount of unreimbursed medical expenses that exceed 7.5% of your AGI (the threshold is typically between 7.5% and 10% of AGI in any normal tax year).

Owners of sole proprietorships, partnerships, S corporations, and some trusts and estates may be eligible for a qualified business income (QBI) deduction, which allows eligible taxpayers to deduct up to 20% of QBI, real estate investment trust (REIT) dividends, and qualified publicly traded partnership (PTP) income. If you are an independent contractor, then your work will qualify for this special deduction.

Step 5: Calculate Taxable Income

For the last step in calculating your taxable income, you will need to take your AGI, calculated above, and subtract all applicable deductions.

As part of the American Rescue Plan, which was signed by President Joe Biden on March 11, 2021, a Senate amendment made $10,200 ($20,400 for married couples filing jointly) of unemployment compensation paid in 2020 tax-free at the federal level for anyone earning less than $150,000. Since states may not conform with the federal exemption, review your state return. If you filed your tax return before March 31, 2021, the IRS would adjust it automatically. The law also includes a provision that student loan forgiveness issued from Jan. 1, 2021, to Dec. 31, 2025, will not be taxable to the recipient.

Taxable Income vs. Nontaxable Income

The IRS considers every type of income to be taxable, but a small number of income streams are nontaxable. For example, if you are a member of a religious organization who has taken a vow of poverty, work for an organization run by that order, and turn your earnings over to the order, then your income is nontaxable. Similarly, if you receive an employee achievement award, then its value is not taxable if certain conditions are met. If someone dies and you receive a life insurance payment, then that is nontaxable income as well.

Different tax agencies define taxable and nontaxable income differently. For example, while the IRS considers lottery winnings to be taxable income in the United States, the Canada Revenue Agency considers most lottery winnings and other unexpected one-time windfalls to be nontaxable.

What Is Considered Taxable Income?

Taxable income includes wages, salaries, bonuses, and tips, as well as investment income and several types of unearned income. Unearned income considered to be taxable income includes canceled debts, alimony payments, child support, government benefits (such as unemployment benefits and disability payments), strike benefits, and lottery payments. Taxable income also includes earnings generated from appreciated assets that have been sold during the year and from dividends and interest income.

How Is Taxable Income Calculated for an Individual Tax Return?

The process starts with determining your filing status (single, married, etc.) and gathering documents for all sources of income (W-2, 1099, etc.). The next step is calculating your adjusted gross income (AGI), which is "above-the-line" adjustments to your gross income, such as contributions to a qualifying individual retirement account (IRA). Then comes the crucial step of calculating your deductions, which can either be standard and/or itemized deductions. Your taxable income is what is left after subtracting all applicable deductions from AGI.

What Are Examples of Nontaxable Income?

The IRS recognizes some income streams as nontaxable. For example, if you are a member of a religious organization who has taken a vow of poverty, work for an organization run by that order, and turn your earnings over to the order, then your income is nontaxable. Similarly, if you receive an employee achievement award, then its value is not taxable if certain conditions are met. If someone dies and you receive a life insurance payment, then that is nontaxable income as well.

Unearned Income

What Is Unearned Income?

Unearned income is income from investments and other sources unrelated to employment. Examples of unearned income include interest from savings accounts, bond interest, alimony, and dividends from stocks. Unearned income, also known as passive income, is income not acquired through work.

Key Takeaways

- Unearned income is not acquired through work or business activities.

- Instead, unearned income is derived from another source, such as an inheritance or passive investments that earn interest or dividends.

- Tax rates on unearned income are different from rates on earned income.

- Before retirement, unearned income can serve as a supplement to earned income; often it is the only source of income in postretirement years.

Understanding Unearned Income

Unearned income differs from earned income, which is income gained from employment, work, or through business activities. Unearned income cannot be used to make contributions to individual retirement accounts (IRAs). According to the Internal Revenue Service (IRS), earned income includes wages, salaries, tips, and self-employment income.

Taxation will differ for earned income and unearned income due to qualitative differences. Additionally, tax rates vary among sources of unearned income. Most unearned income sources are not subject to payroll taxes, and none of it is subject to employment taxes, such as Social Security and Medicare. Therefore, it is crucial for individuals with unearned income to understand the origin and taxation of their income.

Types of Unearned Income

Interest and dividend income are the most common types of unearned income. Money earned in this capacity is unearned income, and the tax paid is considered an unearned income tax.

Interest income, such as interest earned on checking and savings deposit accounts, loans, and certificates of deposit (CDs), is taxed as ordinary income. There are certain exceptions to this rule, including interest earned on municipal bonds, which is exempt from federal income tax.

Dividends, which are income from investments, can be taxed at ordinary tax rates or preferred long-term capital gains tax rates. Investments typically yield dividends payable to shareholders on a regular basis. Dividends may be paid to the investment account monthly, quarterly, annually, or semiannually.

Taxation of dividends is based on whether the dividend is "ordinary" or "qualified." Ordinary dividends are the more generic form of dividend that investors receive from a company. Ordinary dividends are taxed at ordinary tax rates.

Qualified dividends, on the other hand, are taxed at the more favorable capital gains tax rates. Qualified dividends must meet certain criteria. They must be issued by a U.S. corporation or qualified foreign corporation, the investor must own them for at least 60 days out of a 121-day holding period, and they cannot be in a category of dividends otherwise excluded from the qualified dividend classification.

Other sources of unearned income include:

- Retirement accounts—for example, 401(k)s, pensions, and annuities

- Inheritances

- Alimony

- Gifts

- Lottery winnings

- Veterans Affairs (VA) benefits

- Social Security benefits

- Welfare benefits

- Unemployment compensation

- Property income

Unearned income is often a retiree's only source of income.

Benefits of Unearned Income

Unearned income can serve as a supplement to earned income before retirement, and it is often the only source of income in postretirement years. During the accumulation phase, taxes are deferred for many sources of unearned income.

Sources of unearned income that allow a deferment of income tax include 401(k) plans and annuity income. As a result, participants avoid IRS penalties and paying at higher tax rates. Tax advisors often recommend diversifying holdings to even out the effect of taxes on unearned income.

An Example of Unearned Income

Jan invests $50,000 in a CD. The interest she derives from her investment is considered unearned income. She also wins $10,000 on a game show, but she does not get the full amount of her winnings. Why? Because the IRS deducts taxes from it, treating the amount as unearned income.

Income Tax vs. Capital Gains Tax: What's the Difference?

Knowing the difference can help you save money at tax time

Income tax is paid on earnings from employment, interest, dividends, royalties, or self-employment, whether it is in the form of services, money, or property. Capital gains tax is paid on income that derives from the sale or exchange of an asset, such as a stock or property that is categorized as a capital asset.

Key Takeaways

- The U.S. tax system is progressive, with rates ranging from 10% to 37% of a filer's yearly income. Rates rise as income rises.

- For tax purposes, short-term capital gains are treated as ordinary income on assets held for one year or less.

- Long-term capital gains are given preferential tax rates of 0%, 15%, or 20%, depending on your income level.

Income Tax

Your income tax percentage is variable based on your specific tax bracket, and this is dependent on how much income you make throughout the entire calendar year. Tax brackets also vary depending upon whether you file as an individual or jointly with a spouse. For 2020, federal income tax percentages range from 10% to 37% of a person's taxable yearly income after deductions.3

The U.S. has a progressive tax system. Lower-income individuals are taxed at lower rates than higher-income taxpayers on the presumption that those with higher incomes have a greater ability to pay more.4

However, the progressive system is marginal. Segments of income are taxed at different rates. The rates for a single filer in 2020, for example, are as follows:

- 10% on income up to $9,875

- 12% on income over $9,875

- 22% on income over $40,125

- 24% on income over $85,525

- 32% on income over $163,300

- 35% on income over $207,350

- 37% on income over $518,4005

- Thresholds are slightly higher for 2021:

- 10% on income up to $9,950

- 12% on income over $9,950

- 22% on income over $40,525

- 24% on income over $86,375

- 32% on income over $164,925

- 35% on income over $209,425

- 37% on income over $523,6006

Capital Gains Tax

Capital gains tax rates depend on how long the seller owned or held the asset. Short-term capital gains, for assets held for less than a year, are taxed as ordinary income rates. However, if you held an asset for more than a year, then more preferential long-term capital gains apply. These rates are 0%, 15%, or 20%—depending on your income level.

For 2020, a single filer pays 0% on long-term capital gains if that person's income is $40,000 or less. The rate is 15% if the person's income falls under $441,450 and 20% if it is over that amount.

For 2021, the thresholds are slightly higher: You pay 0% on long-term capital gains if you have income of $40,400 or less; 15% if you have income of $445,850 or less; and 20% if your income is greater than $445,850.

An individual must pay taxes at the short-term capital gains rate, which is the same as the ordinary income tax rate, if an asset is held for one year or less.

How to Calculate a Capital Gain

The amount of a capital gain is arrived at by determining your cost basis in the asset. If you purchase a property for $10,000, for example, and spend $1,000 on improvements, then your basis is $11,000. If you then sold the asset for $20,000, your gain is $9,000 ($20,000 minus $11,000).

Income Tax vs. Capital Gains Tax Example

Joe Taxpayer earned $35,000 in 2020. He pays 10% on the first $9,875 income and 12% on the income that comes after that. His total tax liability is $4,003.

If Joe sells an asset that produced a short-term capital gain of $1,000, then his tax liability rises by another $120 (i.e., 12% x $1,000). However, if Joe waits one year and a day to sell, then he pays 0% on the capital gain.

Direct Tax

What Is a Direct Tax?

A direct tax is a tax that a person or organization pays directly to the entity that imposed it. An individual taxpayer, for example, pays direct taxes to the government for various purposes, including income tax, real property tax, private property tax, or taxes on assets.

Key Takeaways

- A direct tax is paid by an individual or organization to the entity that levied the tax.

- Direct taxes include income taxes, property taxes, and taxes on assets.

- There are also indirect taxes, such as sales taxes, wherein a tax is levied on the seller but paid by the buyer.

Direct Tax

Understanding a Direct Tax

Direct taxes in the United States are based on the ability-to-pay principle. This economic principle states that those who have more resources or earn a higher income should bear a greater tax burden. Some critics see that as a disincentive for individuals to work hard and earn more money because the more a person makes, the more taxes they pay.

Direct taxes cannot be passed on to a different person or entity. The individual or organization upon which the tax is levied is responsible for paying it.

A direct tax is the opposite of an indirect tax, wherein the tax is levied on one entity, such as a seller, and paid by another—such as a sales tax paid by the buyer in a retail setting. Both kinds of taxes are important revenue sources for governments.

Examples of indirect taxes include excise duties on fuel, liquor, and cigarettes as well as a value-added tax (VAT), also referred to as a consumption tax.

The History of Direct Taxes

The modern distinction between direct taxes and indirect taxes came about with the ratification of the 16th Amendment to the U.S. Constitution in 1913. Before the 16th Amendment, tax law in the United States was written so that direct taxes had to be directly apportioned to a state's population.1 A state with a population that is 75% of the size of another states, for example, would only be required to pay direct taxes equal to 75% of the larger state's tax bill.

This antiquated verbiage created a situation in which the federal government could not impose many direct taxes, such as a personal income tax, due to apportionment requirements. However, the advent of the 16th Amendment changed the tax code and allowed for the levying of numerous direct and indirect taxes.

Examples of Direct Taxes

Corporate taxes are a good example of direct taxes. If, for example, a manufacturing company reports $1 million in revenue, $500,000 in the cost of goods sold (COGS), and $100,000 in operating costs, its earnings before interest, taxes, depreciation, and amortization (EBITDA) would be $400,000. If the company has no debt, depreciation, or amortization, and has a corporate tax rate of 21%, its direct tax would be $84,000 ($400,000 x 0.21 = $84,000).

An individual's federal income tax is another example of a direct tax. If a person makes $100,000 in a year, for example, and owes the government $20,000 in taxes, that $20,000 would be a direct tax.

Other Types of Direct Taxes

There are a number of other direct taxes that are common in the United States, such as the property taxes that homeowners are required to pay. Those are typically collected by local governments and based on the assessed value of the property. Other types of direct taxes in the U.S. and elsewhere include use taxes (such as vehicle licensing and registration fees), estate taxes, gift taxes, and so-called sin taxes.

Gift Tax

What Is a Gift Tax?

The gift tax is a federal tax applied to an individual giving anything of value to another person. For something to be considered a gift, the receiving party cannot pay the giver full value for the gift, though they may pay an amount less than its full value.

The gift donor must report the gift on their tax return and pay the gift tax. Normally, the recipient does not have to report the gift. Under exceptional circumstances, the recipient may pay the gift tax.

Key Takeaways

- The gift tax is a federal tax levied on a taxpayer who gives money or other items of value, such as property, to someone else.

- The gift tax ranges from 18% to 40%, depending on the size of the gift.

- For 2021, the annual gift exclusion is $15,000 per recipient; the lifetime exemption is $11,700,000 million for a single donor.

- Excluded from the gift tax are gifts made to spouses who are U.S. citizens, to political organizations for use by the organization, and for medical and tuition-related expenses on behalf of the recipient, along with gifts valued at less than the annual exclusion amount.

48

- Gift splitting and gifts in trust are two strategies to avoid incurring the gift tax.

How a Gift Tax Works

The federal gift tax was created to prevent taxpayers from giving money and items of value to others to avoid paying income taxes. The gift tax is applied to the donor to prevent undue hardship and to oblige givers to honor their tax liability, as the Internal Revenue Service (IRS) dubs the giver.

The gift tax can be hefty: Rates range from 18% to 40% on a sliding scale, based on how big the taxable gift is. However, there are a lot of exceptions to the gift tax.

The following are not subject to gift tax:

- Gifts to the donor's spouse. An unlimited amount can be gifted tax-free if the spouse is a U.S. citizen. If the spouse is not a U.S. citizen, then tax-free gifts are limited to an annually adjusted value ($159,000 in 2021)

- Gifts to a political organization for its use

- Medical and educational expenses—payments made by a donor to a person or an organization, such as a college, doctor, or hospital

- Gifts to a charitable organization

- Gifts that are valued at less than the annual gift tax exclusion rate for that year (see below)

Gift Tax Exclusions

The gift tax is only triggered on gifts above a certain amount. Sums below that amount—whether actual cash or the value of the gift—are what is called "excluded" from the gift tax. There are two types of exclusions: annual and lifetime.

In 2021, the annual exclusion is $15,000 per recipient.4 This means that an individual can give another individual $15,000 or less per year without incurring a gift tax. The annual gift tax exclusion is per recipient, not per donor. So, one person could bestow several gifts worth up to $15,000 to different people without triggering the gift tax.

The lifetime exclusion is the total sum that an individual can give over the course of their life. Adjusted annually for inflation, this exclusion is $11,700,000 in 2021. That means the donor can gift up to this amount before the gift tax is applied.5 Annual limits still apply; the lifetime exemption applies to amounts *over and above* annual exclusions.

If your gift to any single recipient exceeds the annual maximum ($15,000 in 2021), then you will not necessarily owe gift tax, because it still may be under the lifetime gift tax exclusion amount. But you will have to report the gift on your tax return, by filing IRS Form 709.

Gift Tax Strategies

There are strategies for avoiding or minimizing the gift tax.

Gift Splitting

Being married allows you to double your gifts. Remember, the annual exclusion applies to the amount of gift that an individual can give a recipient. That means that even if they file a joint tax return, spouses can *each* give $15,000 to the same recipient—effectively raising that gift to $30,000 per year without triggering the gift tax.

This strategy is known as "gift splitting" and enables wealthy couples to give substantial annual gifts to children, grandchildren, and others.3 This gift can be on top of, say, tuition paid directly to a grandchild's school or college—which is exempted outright from the gift tax.

Gift in Trust

Donors can give gifts more than the annual exclusion without paying taxes by establishing a special type of trust—the Crummey trust is the usual arrangement—to receive and distribute the funds.

The gift tax exclusion usually does not apply to money distributed by trusts. But a Crummey trust allows the beneficiary to withdraw the assets within a limited time—say, 90 days or six months. This gives the beneficiary what the IRS calls a "present interest" in the trust—and this sort of distribution can qualify as a nontaxable gift. Of course, the recipient can only take out a sum equal to the gift given to the trust.

Under exceptional circumstances, like 529 college savings plan contributions, you can gift more than the annual $15,000 without reducing your lifetime gift tax exemption. You report this single large gift as being spread over five years on your tax return, filing the form each year. The only catch: You cannot make any additional gifts to the same recipient during this period. If you do, then it *will* be applied to your $11.7 million lifetime exclusion.

Gift Tax Return

The federal gift tax return is known as Form 709. It must be filed under certain conditions by the donor of a gift. Gift recipients normally do not have to report gifts—though they may pay the gift tax, or a percentage of it, on the giver's behalf (in which case they would have to file the form).

Individuals who give a gift that exceeds the annual or lifetime exempt gift limit established by the IRS must fill out and submit Form 709. This form is due on the same date as the individual's tax return (Form 1040), which is typically April 15 of the year after the gift was made.

Form 709 includes calculations for how much gift tax, if any, is owed. But filing Form 709 does not necessarily mean that you pay the gift tax. If you have given a gift that exceeds the annual exclusion maximum ($15,000 in 2021) but is still under the lifetime maximum ($11,700,000 in 2021), then you will not trigger the gift tax. But you still must report the gift.

Examples of the Gift Tax

1. Taxpayer A gives $20,000 to each of the five recipients in 2020. Because the annual exclusion limit is $15,000 per person, $25,000 of the total amount given is not excluded. However, the non-excluded amount reduces the lifetime exemption amount. So, after making these gifts, Taxpayer A has $11,555,000 remaining of the exemption to give before paying gift taxes.

2. A grandmother who wants to encourage her granddaughter's going to medical school pays the school $20,000 for a year's tuition. That same year, she also directly gives the girl $15,000 for books, supplies, and equipment. Neither payment is reportable for gift tax purposes—the tuition is excluded outright, and the $15,000 is the maximum allowed under the annual exclusion. If Grandma had sent the future physician $30,000 and the girl had paid the school, then the grandmother would have made a reportable (but not taxable) gift in the amount of $15,000 ($30,000 less the annual exclusion of $15,000), which would have reduced her $11,700,000 lifetime exclusion by $15,000.

How Much Is the Gift Tax?

The gift tax is applied on a sliding scale, depending on the size of the gift. It only kicks in on gifts beyond a certain threshold established by the IRS. First, a flat amount is assessed; additional tax is then levied at a rate that ranges from 18% to 40%.

How Much Can I Gift Someone Tax Free?

You can give someone (or more than one recipient) up to $15,000 each year without triggering the gift tax. Over your lifetime, you can give gifts totaling $11,700,000.

Does the Receiver of a Gift Pay Tax?

The person receiving a gift usually is not required to pay gift tax. The recipient can opt to do so, though, especially if the amount would put the donor over their lifetime gift tax exclusion.

How Much Can I Gift My Child?

You can gift your child or grandchild the same amount that you can gift other relatives or friends without incurring the gift tax, namely:

- $15,000 annually per child

- $11,700,000 over the course of your lifetime

These figures are for 2021. The IRS regularly adjusts these maximums for inflation.

Since the $15,000 threshold applies to one donor, a married couple can each give that amount to the same child, resulting in an annual $30,000 gift.

The Bottom Line

The gift tax is a federal levy that applies when you give to another individual or individuals, without charge, a sum of cash or assets—either tangible or intangible—that have intrinsic worth. It is imposed on the donor rather than on the receiver.

However, the gift tax has been devised in such a way that very few people end up paying it. Numerous types of gifts are exempted, including anything to a spouse. In addition, you can give a seven-figure sum over the course of your life before the gift tax is triggered—and even then, it applies to the amount above that threshold.

State Income Tax

What Is State Income Tax?

State income tax is a direct tax levied by a state on your income. Income is what you earned in or from the state. In your state of residence, it may mean all your income earned anywhere. Like federal tax, state income tax is self-assessed, which means taxpayers file required state tax returns.

Key Takeaways

- As of 2021, 41 states and Washington, D.C., impose an income tax.

- State tax laws, rates, procedures, and forms vary among states.

- You must file a state tax return for every tax-levying state in which you earn income, though only the state in which you live can tax all your income.

Understanding State Income Tax

Tax laws, rates, procedures, and forms vary widely from state to state. Filing deadlines also vary, but for individuals, state Tax Day usually falls on the same day as federal Tax Day, which is typically April 15. However, state filing deadlines were updated for the 2019 and 2020 tax years due to the COVID-19 crisis.

Taxpayers must file tax returns in each state and each year that they earn an income more than the state's filing threshold. Many states conform to federal rules for income and deduction recognition. Some may even require a copy of the taxpayer's federal income tax return to be filed with the state income tax return.

As of the 2021 tax year, eight states have no income tax: Alaska, Florida, Nevada, South Dakota, Tennessee, Texas, Washington, and Wyoming. New Hampshire taxes unearned income, such as interest and dividends, but it will end the practice as of Jan. 1, 2024.

Forty-one states and Washington, D.C., do have a state income tax.3 If you live in a state that levies an income tax, avoidance of it by working in a no-income-tax state is not possible. Your home state will continue to tax the income even though your earnings were made in a no-income-tax state.

Just like the Internal Revenue Service (IRS), states require taxpayers with income that is not subject to withholding, such as business or self-employment income, to estimate their annual tax liability and pay it in four quarterly installments. States will impose penalties and interest on taxpayers who fail to file and pay state income taxes on time and in full. Many taxpayers get a measure of relief knowing that states are barred from adjusting their state income taxes once the applicable statute of limitations has expired.

If you have income that is not subject to withholding, such as business or self-employment income, you must estimate your annual tax liability and pay it to the state in four quarterly installments.

Special Considerations

Working and living in different states

Most taxpayers live and work in a single state and file a resident state income tax return there. However, taxpayers who earn wages or income in one or more states other than where they live may be required to file state income tax returns in those states as well—unless, of course, a state is a no-income-tax state.

If, for example, you are an actor living in Jersey City, N.J., and you work on Broadway in New York City, do TV or movies in Los Angeles, and play a regional theater gig in Chicago, then you must pay taxes in the states of New Jersey, New York, California, and Illinois. Furthermore, your tax home is the general area of your main place of business. If you spend most of your time working on Broadway, then your tax home would be New York.

According to the IRS, to determine your main place of business, you must consider the length of time you spend in the location, the degree of business activity occurring in the location, and the relative significance of the financial return from each location. However, the most crucial factor is the length of time that you spend in each location.

Returns in a state where you do not have a domicile will be filed as a nonresident or a part-year resident. Some states, often those that border each other, have entered into reciprocal agreements not to tax the same income. If no understanding is in force and your income will be taxed multiple times, then credits or deductions may be available as you file your state income tax return. If you telecommute, the rules can be even more complex. In such cases, it is advisable to check with a tax expert before filing your taxes.

In an interesting situation, the state of New Hampshire sued the state of Massachusetts in October 2020 in response to a law enacted by Massachusetts earlier that year. Massachusetts adopted an emergency law that would allow the state to tax employees who previously commuted into the state but, because of closed offices during the COVID-19 crisis, were working remotely. This specifically impacted employees who were New Hampshire residents. New Hampshire does not tax wages, but Massachusetts has a 5% state income tax. In June 2021, the U.S. Supreme Court rejected New Hampshire's challenge to the new Massachusetts law.

Depending upon the residency rules of the home state, expats may also still have a state filing requirement.

State income taxes on businesses

Some states impose an income tax on corporations, partnerships, and certain trusts and estates. These states frequently offer lower corporate rates and special exemptions to attract businesses to locate there. States cannot impose an income tax on a U.S. or foreign corporation unless it has a substantial connection, called a "nexus."

Requirements for a nexus are different among states, but they include earning income in the state, owning, or renting property there, employing people there, or having capital assets or property there.7 Even then, the income taxes imposed are apportioned and nondiscriminatory and require that other constitutional standards are met.

Tax Bracket

What Is a Tax Bracket?

A tax bracket refers to a range of incomes subject to a certain income tax rate. Tax brackets result in a progressive tax system, in which taxation progressively increases as an individual's income grows. Low incomes fall into tax brackets with low-income tax rates, while higher earnings fall into brackets with higher rates.

Key Takeaways

- There are currently seven federal tax brackets in the U.S., with rates ranging from 10% to 37%.

- The U.S. tax system is progressive, with lower brackets paying lower rates and higher brackets paying higher ones.

- Unless your income lands you in the lowest tax bracket, you are charged at multiple rates as your income rises, rather than just at the rate of the bracket into which you fall.

Understanding Tax Brackets

In the U.S., the Internal Revenue Service (IRS) uses a progressive tax system, meaning taxpayers will pay the lowest rate of tax on the first level of taxable income in their bracket, a higher rate on the next level, and so on. Currently, there are seven federal tax brackets, each assigned a different rate, ranging from 10% to 37%, with the dollar ranges in each varying for single filers, married joint filers (and qualifying widow[er]s), married filing separately filers, and head of household filers, resulting in 28 effective tax brackets.

When determining which tax bracket to use, a taxpayer should first calculate their taxable income (earned and investment income minus adjustments and deductions).

Let us take an example based on the rates for tax year 2020. Single filers who have less than $9,875 in taxable income are subject to a 10% income tax rate (the lowest bracket). Single filers who earn more than this amount will have their first $9,875 in earnings taxed at 10%, but their earnings past that cutoff point and up to $40,125 are subjected to a 12% rate, the next bracket. Earnings from $40,125 to $84,200 are taxed at 22%, the third bracket. And so on.

Tax brackets are adjusted each year for inflation, using the Consumer Price Index (CPI).

Single Taxable Income Tax Brackets and Rates for 2020

Taxable Income Bracket	Tax Owed
$0 to $9,875	10% of taxable income
$9,876–$40,125	$987.50 plus 12% of the excess over $9,875
$40,126–$85,525	$4,617.50 plus 22% of the excess over $40,125
$85,526–$163,300	$14,605.50 plus 24% of the excess over $85,525
$163,301–$207,350	$33,271.50 plus 32% of the excess over $163,300
$207,351–$518,400	$47,367.50 plus 35% of the excess over $207,350
Over $518,400	$156,235 plus 37% of the excess over $518,400

Married Filing Jointly Taxable Income Tax Brackets and Rates for 2020

Taxable Income Bracket	Tax Owed
$0 to $19,750	10% of taxable income
$19,751–$80,250	$1,975 plus 12% of the excess over $19,750
$80,251–$171,050	$9,235 plus 22% of the excess over $80,250
$171,051–$326,600	$29,211 plus 24% of the excess over $171,050
$326,601–$414,700	$66,543 plus 32% of the excess over $326,600
$414,701–$622,050	$94,735 plus 35% of the excess over $414,700
Over $622,050	$167,307.50 plus 37% of the excess over $622,050

Tax Rates vs. Tax Brackets

People often refer to their tax brackets and their tax rates as the same thing, but they are not. A tax rate is a percentage at which income is taxed; each tax bracket has a different tax rate (10%, 12%, 22%, etc.), referred to as the marginal rate. However, most taxpayers—all except those who fall squarely into the minimum bracket—have income that is taxed progressively, so they are subject to several different rates, beyond the nominal one of their tax brackets. Your tax bracket does not necessarily reflect how much you will pay in total taxes. The term for this is the effective tax rate. Here is how it works.

Consider the following tax responsibility for a single filer with a taxable income of $50,000 in 2020:

- The first $9,875 is taxed at 10%: $9,875 × 0.10 = $987.50

- Then $9,876 to $40,125, or $30,250, is taxed at 12%: $30,250 × 0.12 = $3,630

- Finally, the top $9,875 (what is left of the $50,000 income) is taxed at 22%: $10,524 × 0.22 = $2,172.501

Add the taxes owed in each of the brackets, and you get $987.50 + $3,630 + $2,172.50 = $6,790.

Result: This individual's effective tax rate is approximately 13.5% of income.

Pros and Cons of Tax Brackets

Tax brackets—and the progressive tax system that they create—contrast with a flat tax structure, in which all individuals are taxed at the same rate, regardless of their income levels.

Pros

- Higher-income individuals are more able to pay income taxes and keep a good living standard.

- Low-income individuals pay less, leaving them more to support themselves.

- Tax deductions and credits give high-income individuals tax relief, while rewarding useful behavior, such as donating to charity.

Cons

- Wealthy people end up paying a disproportionate amount of taxes.

- Brackets make the wealthy focus on finding tax loopholes that result in many underpaying their taxes, depriving the government of revenue.

- Progressive taxation leads to reduced personal savings.

Positives

Proponents of tax brackets and progressive tax systems contend that individuals with high incomes are better able to pay income taxes while maintaining a high standard of living, while low-income individuals—those who struggle to meet their basic needs—should be subject to less taxation.

They stress that it is only fair that wealthy taxpayers pay more in taxes than the poor and the middle class, offsetting the inequality of income distribution. That makes the progressive taxation system "progressive" in both senses of the word: It rises in stages and is designed with help for lower-income taxpayers in mind. Taxes you pay on 401(k) withdrawals, for instance, are also based on tax brackets.

Supporters maintain that this system can generate higher revenues for governments and still be fair by letting taxpayers lower their tax bill through adjustments, such as tax deductions or tax credits for outlays such as charitable contributions.

The higher income that taxpayers realize can then be funneled back into the economy. Furthermore, the use of tax brackets has an automatic stabilizing effect on an individual's after-tax income, as a decrease in funds is counteracted by a decrease in the tax rate, leaving the individual with a less substantial decrease.

Negatives

Opponents of tax brackets and progressive tax schedules argue that everyone, regardless of income or economic status, is equal under the law and that there should be no discrimination between rich and poor. They also point out that progressive taxation can lead to a substantial discrepancy between the amount of tax that wealthy people pay and the amount of government representation that they receive. Some even go on to point out that citizens get only one vote per person regardless of the personal or even national percentage of tax that they pay.

Opponents also claim that higher taxation at higher income levels can (and does) lead to the wealthy spending money to exploit tax law loopholes and find creative ways to shelter earnings and assets—often with the result that they end up paying less in taxes than the less well-off, depriving the government of revenue. (American companies that relocate their headquarters abroad, for example, frequently do so to avoid U.S. corporate taxes.)

They also assert that the progressive system has historically led to reduced personal savings rates among taxpayers. After spiking to 12% in December 2012, the personal savings rate suddenly dropped to 5.8% by February 2013. However, as of February 2021, the rate had resurged to 13.6%.

History of Federal Tax Brackets

Tax brackets have existed in the U.S. tax code since the inception of the very first income tax, when the Union government passed the Revenue Act of 1861 to help fund its war against the Confederacy. A second revenue act in 1862 established the first two tax brackets: 3% for annual incomes from $600 to $10,000, and 5% on incomes above $10,000.3 The original four filing statuses were single, married filing jointly, married filing separately, and head of household, though rates were the same regardless of tax status.

In 1872, Congress rescinded the income tax. It did not reappear until the 16th Amendment to the Constitution—which established Congress' right to levy a federal income tax—was ratified in 1913. That same year, Congress enacted a 1% income tax for individuals earning more than $3,000 a year and couples earning more than $4,000, with a graduated surtax of 1% to 7% on incomes from $20,000 and up.

Over the years, the number of tax brackets has fluctuated. When the federal income tax began in 1913, there were seven tax brackets. In 1918, the number mushroomed to 78 brackets, ranging from 6% to 77%.7 In 1944, the top rate hit 91%.8 But it was brought back down to 70% in 1964 by then-President Lyndon B. Johnson.9 In 1981, then-President Ronald Reagan initially brought the top rate down to 50%.

Then, in the Tax Reform Act of 1986, brackets were simplified, and the rates reduced so that, in 1988, there were only two brackets: 15% and 28%.11 This system lasted only until 1991, when a third bracket of 31% was added. Since then, additional brackets have been implemented, and we have come full circle and are back to seven brackets, a structure that was retained by the 2017 Tax Cuts and Jobs Act (TCJA).

State Tax Brackets

Some states have no income tax: Alaska, Florida, Nevada, South Dakota, Texas, Washington, and Wyoming. Tennessee previously only taxed investment and interest income, but that practice was repealed as of Jan. 1, 2021. Meanwhile, New Hampshire's tax on investment and interest income will expire in 2024.

In 2020, nine states have a flat rate structure, with a single rate applying to a resident's income: Colorado (4.63%), Illinois (4.95%), Indiana (3.23%), Kentucky (5.0%), Massachusetts (5.05%), Michigan (4.25%), North Carolina (5.25%), Pennsylvania (3.07%), and Utah (4.95%).16

In other states, the number of tax brackets varies from three to as many as nine (in Missouri and California) and even 12 (in Hawaii). The marginal tax rates in these brackets also vary considerably. California has the highest, maxing out at 12.3%.

State income tax regulations may or may not mirror federal rules. For example, some states allow residents to use the federal personal exemption and standard deduction amounts for figuring state income tax, while others have their own exemption and standard deduction amounts.

How to Find Your Tax Bracket

There are numerous online sources to find your specific federal income tax bracket. The IRS makes available a variety of information, including annual tax tables that provide highly detailed tax filing statuses in increments of $50 of taxable income up to $100,000.

Other websites provide tax bracket calculators that do the math for you, as long as you know your filing status and taxable income. Your tax bracket can shift from year to year, depending on inflation adjustments and changes in your income and status, so it is worth checking on an annual basis.

Tax Bracket FAQs

What Are the Federal Tax Brackets for Tax Year 2020?

The top tax rate remains 37% for individual single taxpayers with incomes greater than $518,400 ($622,050 for married couples filing jointly). Below are the other brackets:

- 35%, for incomes over $207,350 ($414,700 for married couples filing jointly)

- 32%, for incomes over $163,300 ($326,600 for married couples filing jointly)

- 24%, for incomes over $85,525 ($171,050 for married couples filing jointly)

- 22%, for incomes over $40,125 ($80,250 for married couples filing jointly)

- 12%, for incomes over $9,875 ($19,750 for married couples filing jointly)

The lowest rate is 10% for incomes of single individuals with incomes of $9,875 or less ($19,750 for married couples filing jointly).

Did Tax Tables Change for 2021?

Yes. Each year, the IRS adjusts the tax brackets to account for inflation. Below are the income thresholds for tax year 2021.

The top tax rate remains 37% for individual single taxpayers with incomes greater than $523,600 ($628,300 for married couples filing jointly). Below are the other rates:

- 35%, for incomes over $209,425 ($418,850 for married couples filing jointly)

- 32%, for incomes over $164,925 ($329,850 for married couples filing jointly)

- 24%, for incomes over $86,375 ($172,750 for married couples filing jointly)

- 22%, for incomes over $40,525 ($81,050 for married couples filing jointly)

- 12%, for incomes over $9,950 ($19,900 for married couples filing jointly)

The lowest rate is 10% for incomes of single individuals with incomes of $9,950 or less ($19,900 for married couples filing jointly).

How Much Can I Earn Before I Pay 40% Tax?

For tax year 2020, the highest earners in the U.S. pay a 37% tax rate on all income made beyond $518,400 ($622,050 for married couples filing jointly).

How Do I Calculate My Tax Bracket?

To estimate which tax bracket your earnings will fall under, you could do the math yourself by using the calculation above or visit the IRS website, which provides highly detailed tax filing statuses in increments of $50 of taxable income up to $100,000.

Value-Added Tax (VAT)

What Is a Value-Added Tax (VAT)?

A value-added tax (VAT) is collected on a product at every stage of its production during which value is added to it, from its initial production to the point of sale. The amount of VAT that the user pays is based on the cost of the product, less any costs of materials used in the product that have already been taxed at a previous stage.

The value-added tax is a type of consumption tax.

Key Takeaways

- A value-added tax, or VAT, is added to a product at every point on the supply chain where value is added to it.

- Advocates of VATs claim that they raise government revenues without punishing the wealthy by charging them more through an income tax. Critics say that VATs place an undue economic burden on lower-income taxpayers.

- Although many industrialized countries have value-added taxation, the United States is not one of them.

Understanding the VAT

Value-added taxation is based on consumption rather than income. In contrast to a progressive income tax, which levies more taxes on the wealthy, the VAT is charged equally on every purchase. More than 160 countries use a VAT system. It is most found in the European Union.

Nevertheless, it is not without controversy.

Advocates say a VAT raises government revenues without charging wealthy taxpayers more, as income taxes do. It also is considered simpler and more standardized than a traditional sales tax, with fewer compliance issues.

Critics argue that a VAT is a regressive tax that places an undue economic burden on lower-income consumers while increasing the bureaucratic burden on businesses.

Both critics and proponents of a VAT argue it as an alternative to an income tax. That is not necessarily the case. Great Britain, for example, has both an income tax and a VAT.

How a VAT Works

A VAT is levied on the gross margin at each point in the process of manufacturing, distributing, and selling an item. The tax is assessed and collected at each stage. That is different from a sales tax system, in which the tax is assessed and paid only by the consumer at the very end of the supply chain.

Say, for example, a candy called Dulce is manufactured and sold in the imaginary country of Alexia. Alexia has a 10% VAT.

Here is how the VAT would work:

1. Dulce's manufacturer buys the raw materials for $2, plus a VAT of 20 cents—payable to the government of Alexia—for a total price of $2.20.

2. The manufacturer then sells Dulce to a retailer for $5 plus a VAT of 50 cents, for a total of $5.50. The manufacturer renders only 30 cents to Alexia, which is the total VAT at this point, minus the prior VAT charged by the raw material supplier. Note that the 30 cents also equal 10% of the manufacturer's gross margin of $3.

3. Finally, a retailer sells Dulce to consumers for $10 plus a VAT of $1, for a total of $11. The retailer renders 50 cents to Alexia, which is the total VAT at this point ($1), minus the prior 50-cent VAT charged by the manufacturer. The 50 cents also represent 10% of the retailer's gross margin on Dulce.

History of the VAT

Most industrialized countries that make up the Organization for Economic Cooperation and Development (OECD) have a VAT system. The United States remains the only notable exception.[1]

Most industrial countries with a VAT adopted their systems in the 1980s. Results have been mixed, but VAT countries in general do not enjoy small budget deficits or low government debt. According to one International Monetary Fund (IMF) study, any nation that switches to VAT initially feels the negative impact of reduced tax revenues despite greater revenue potential down the road.[2]

VAT has earned a negative connotation in some parts of the world, even hurting its proponents politically. In the Philippines, for example, Sen. Ralph Recto, a chief proponent of VAT in the early 2000s,[3] was voted out of office by the electorate when he ran for reelection.[4] However, in the years that followed its implementation, the population eventually accepted the tax. Recto ended up finding his way back to the Senate, where he became the proponent of an expanded VAT.

In 2009, France famously implemented a huge cut in its VAT rate—almost 75%, from a 19.6% rate to a 5.5% rate. Since then, the nation has raised its standard VAT rate to 20%, with reduced rates for some products.

Industrial nations that have adopted a VAT system have had mixed results, with one study noting that any country making the switch feels an initial negative impact from reduced tax revenues.

Value-Added Tax vs. Sales Tax

VATs and sales taxes can raise the same amount of revenue. The differences lie in the point at which the money is paid and by whom. Here is an example that assumes (again) a VAT of 10%:

- A farmer sells wheat to a baker for 30 cents. The baker pays 33 cents; the extra 3 cents represent the VAT, which the farmer sends to the government.

- The baker uses the wheat to make bread and sells a loaf to a local supermarket for 70 cents. The supermarket pays 77 cents, including a 7-cent VAT. The baker sends 4 cents to the government; the other 3 cents were paid by the farmer.

- Finally, the supermarket sells the loaf of bread to a customer for $1. Of the $1.10 paid by the customer, or the base price plus the VAT, the supermarket sends 3 cents to the government.

Just as it would with a traditional 10% sales tax, the government receives 10 cents on a $1 sale. The VAT differs in that it is paid at different stops along the supply chain; the farmer pays 3 cents, the baker pays 4 cents, and the supermarket pays 3 cents.

However, a VAT offers advantages over a national sales tax. It is much easier to track. The exact tax levied at each step of production is known.

With a sales tax, the entire amount is rendered after the sale, making it difficult to allocate to specific production stages. Additionally, because the VAT only taxes each value addition—not the sale of a product itself—assurance is provided that the same product is not double taxed.

Special Considerations

There has been much debate in the United States about replacing the current income tax system with a federal VAT. Advocates claim it would increase government revenue, help fund essential social services, and reduce the federal deficit. Most recently, a VAT was advocated by 2020 presidential candidate Andrew Yang.

In 1992, the Congressional Budget Office (CBO) conducted an economic study on implementing a VAT. At the time, the CBO concluded that a VAT would add only $150 billion in annual revenue, or less than 3% of national output.7 If you adjust those numbers to 2020 dollars, it comes out to just under $275 billion, or 3% of the third quarter of 2019 gross domestic product (GDP).

Using these approximations, it can be estimated that a VAT might raise between $250 billion and $500 billion in revenue for the government.

Of course, these figures do not account for all the outside impacts of a VAT system. A VAT would change the structure of production in the United States, as not all firms will be equally able to absorb the increased input costs.

It is unknown if the additional revenue would be used as an excuse to borrow more money—historically, proven to be the case in Europe—or reduce taxes in other areas (potentially making the VAT budget neutral).

The Baker Institute for Public Policy at Rice University, in conjunction with Ernst & Young, conducted a macroeconomic analysis of the VAT in 2010. The principal findings were that the VAT would reduce retail spending by $2.5 trillion over 10 years, the economy could lose up to 850,000 jobs in the first year alone, and the VAT would have "significant redistribution effects" that would harm current workers.

Three years later, in a 2013 Brookings Institution report, William Gale and Benjamin Harris proposed a VAT to help solve the country's fiscal problems coming out of the Great Recession. They calculated that a 5% VAT could reduce the deficit by $1.6 trillion over 10 years and raise revenues without distorting savings and investment choices.

Pros and Cons of a VAT

In addition to the fiscal arguments, proponents of a VAT in the United States suggest that replacing the current income tax system with a federal VAT would have other positive effects.

Pros

- Substituting a VAT for other taxes such as the income tax would close tax loopholes.

- A VAT provides a stronger incentive to earn more money than a progressive income tax does.

Cons

- A VAT creates higher costs for businesses.

- It encourages tax evasion.

- Passed-along costs lead to higher prices—a particular burden on low-income consumers.

Pro: Closing Tax Loopholes

Proponents argue that a VAT would not only greatly simplify the complex federal tax code and increase the efficiency of the Internal Revenue Service (IRS) but also make it much more difficult to avoid paying taxes.

A VAT would collect revenue on all goods sold in the United States, including online purchases.

Pro: A Stronger Incentive to Earn

If a VAT supplants U.S. income tax, it eliminates the disincentive-to-succeed complaint levied against progressive tax systems: Citizens get to keep more of the money that they make and are only taxed when purchasing goods.

This change not only confers a stronger incentive to earn; it also encourages saving and discourages frivolous spending (at least theoretically).

Con: Higher Costs for Businesses

Opponents note potential drawbacks of a VAT, including increased costs for business owners throughout the chain of production. Because VAT is calculated at every step of the sales process, bookkeeping alone results in a bigger burden for a company, which then passes on the additional cost to the consumer.

It becomes more complex when transactions are not only local but also international. Different countries may have different interpretations on how to calculate the tax. This not only adds another layer to the bureaucracy but also can result in unnecessary transaction delays.

Con: Encouraging Tax Evasion

While a VAT system may be simpler to maintain, it is costlier to implement. Tax evasion can continue, and even be widespread, if the public does not give it wholehearted support.

Smaller businesses can evade paying VAT by asking their customers if they require a receipt, adding that the price of the product or service being purchased is lower if no official receipt is issued.

Con: Conflicts Between State and Local Governments

In the United States, a federal VAT could also create conflicts with state and local governments across the country, which currently set their own sales taxes.

Con: Higher Prices

Critics note that consumers typically wind up paying higher prices with a VAT. While the VAT theoretically spreads the tax burden on the added value of a good as it moves through the supply chain from raw material to final product, in practice, the increased costs are typically passed along to the consumer.

What Does a Value-Added Tax Do?

A value-added tax (VAT) is a flat tax levied on an item. It is similar in some respects to a sales tax, except that with a sales tax, the full amount owed to the government is paid by the consumer at the point of sale. With a VAT, portions of the tax amount are paid by different parties to a transaction.

Does the United States Have a Value-Added Tax?

No, the United States has no VAT. The federal government raises money primarily through the income tax system. The states and local governments establish and collect their own sales taxes. Local governments rely primarily on property taxes.

Who Benefits from a VAT and Who Doesn't?

Wealthier consumers could come out ahead if a VAT replaced the income tax. As with other flat taxes, a VAT's impact would be felt less by the wealthy and more by the poor, who spend most of their income on necessities.

In short, lower-income consumers would pay a much higher proportion of their earnings in taxes with a VAT system, critics including the Tax Policy Center charge.

Can the Negative Effects of a VAT on Lower-Income People Be Fixed?

Yes, to some extent. A government can exclude certain basic household goods, food products, or medicines from the VAT, or it can charge a lower VAT rate. It also can provide rebates or credits to low-income citizens to offset the effects of the tax.

Wealth Tax

What Is Wealth Tax?

Wealth tax is a tax based on the market value of assets owned by a taxpayer. Although many developed countries choose to tax wealth, the United States has historically relied on taxing annual income to raise revenue.

Recently, however, the immense and increasing disparity in wealth in the United States—as of 2018, the wealthiest 10% owned 70% of the country's wealth, while the richest 1% owned 32%, according to the Federal Reserve Board—prompted politicians such as Sen. Bernie Sanders and Sen. Elizabeth Warren to propose a wealth tax, in addition to the income tax, in the run-up to the 2020 presidential election in which they were both candidates. In March 2021, Warren introduced S.510, a revised version of her earlier proposal, to impose a tax on the net worth of very wealthy individuals.

Key Takeaways

- A wealth tax is a tax levied on the net reasonable value of a taxpayer's assets.

- A wealth tax applies to the net reasonable value of all or some of a variety of asset types held by a taxpayer, including cash, bank deposits, shares, fixed assets, personal cars, real property, pension plans, money funds, owner-occupied housing, and trusts.

- France, Portugal, and Spain all have wealth taxes.

- U.S. politicians have proposed adding a wealth tax to distribute the tax burden more fairly in a society with immense economic disparity.

Understanding Wealth Taxes

A wealth tax also may be called "capital tax" or "equity tax" and is imposed on the wealth possessed by individuals. The tax usually applies to a person's net worth, which is assets minus liabilities. These assets include (but are not limited to) cash, bank deposits, shares, fixed assets, personal cars, real property, pension plans, money funds, owner-occupied housing, and trusts. An ad valorem tax on real estate and an intangible tax on financial assets are both examples of a wealth tax.

Countries that impose wealth taxes also impose income and other taxes.

Not all countries impose a wealth tax. France, Portugal, and Spain are examples of countries that do, but Austria, Denmark, Finland, Germany, Iceland, Luxembourg, and Sweden have abolished it in recent years. In the United States, federal and state governments do not impose wealth taxes. Instead, the U.S. imposes annual income and property taxes. However, some consider the property tax a form of wealth tax, as the government taxes the same asset year after year. The U.S. also imposes an estate tax on the death of individuals owning high-value estates. However, in 2019, that levy contributed only 0.5% of total U.S. tax revenues.

Examples of a Wealth Tax

In effect, a wealth tax impacts the net value of the assets accumulated over time and owned by a taxpayer as of the end of each tax year. An income tax impacts the flow of the additions in value that a taxpayer realizes, whether as earnings, investment returns such as interest, dividends, or rents, and/or profits on disposition of assets during the year.

Let us look at an example of how the wealth tax differs from income tax. Assume a single taxpayer earns $120,000 annually and falls in the 24% tax bracket. That individual's liability for the year will be 24% x $120,000 = $28,800. What is the tax liability if the government taxes wealth instead of income? If the taxpayer's assessed net worth is $450,000 and the wealth tax is 24%, then the tax debt for the year will be 24% x $450,000 = $108,000.

Annual wealth tax rates are significantly lower than annual income tax rates. In France, for example, the wealth tax used to apply to total worldwide assets. As of 2020, however, it only applied to real estate assets worth more than €800,000. If the value of those assets falls between €800,000 and €1,300,000, then it is subject to a 0.5% tax. Rates continue to rise at graduated thresholds—0.7%, 1%, 1.25%—until, finally, real estate assets over €10,000,000 are taxed at 1.5%. A wealth tax cap limits total taxes to 75% of income. In Spain, as of 2019, a resident is affected by the wealth tax, which ranges from 0.2% to 3.45% if the value of their worldwide assets is above €700,000.

If a taxpayer is not a resident of a particular country, then the wealth tax only applies to their holdings in that country.

S.510: Senator Warren's Wealth Tax

Here is what Senator Warren is proposing, beginning with the 2023 tax year:

- Taxpayers subject to the wealth tax: Those whose net assets, i.e., assets minus debt, are valued over $50 billion, based on their 2022 valuation.

- Tax rate: 1% on net assets valued over $50 million and up to $1 billion; 2% on net assets more than $1 billion.2 The threshold for the net asset base is higher than typical European wealth taxes.

- Assets subject to tax: all types of assets—anything that the wealthy person owns, including stock, real estate, boats, art, and more.

- Revenue effect: S.510 is estimated to raise up to $3.75 trillion over 10 years and to apply to approximately 100,000 households.

Upon introduction, the bill had seven Senate co-sponsors: Sens. Edward Markey, Kirsten Gillibrand, Sheldon Whitehouse, Brian Schatz, Bernie Sanders, Jeff Merkley, and Mazie Hirono. An eighth senator, Alex Padilla, later became another co-sponsor. Two House co-sponsors, Reps. Pramila Jayapal and Brenda F. Boyle, support a companion bill in that chamber. All are Democrats.

Pros and Cons of a Wealth Tax

Proponents of wealth taxes believe this type of tax is more equitable than an income tax alone, particularly in societies with significant wealth disparity. They believe that a system that raises government revenue from both the income and the net assets of taxpayers promotes fairness and equality by considering taxpayers' overall economic status, and thus, their ability to pay tax. Critics allege that wealth taxes discourage the accumulation of wealth, which they contend drives economic growth. They also emphasize that wealth taxes are difficult to administer.

Administration and enforcement of a wealth tax present challenges not typically entailed in income taxes. The difficulty of determining the fair market value of assets that lack publicly available prices leads to valuation disputes between taxpayers and tax authorities. Uncertainty about valuation also could tempt some wealthy individuals to try tax evasion.

Illiquid assets present another issue for a wealth tax. Owners of significant illiquid assets may lack ready cash to pay their wealth tax liability. This creates a problem for people who have low incomes and low liquid savings but own a high-value, illiquid asset, such as a home. For a similar example, a farmer who earns little but owns land with a high value may have trouble producing the money to pay a wealth tax.

Some accommodations may be feasible to address administrative and cash flow issues—for example, allowing tax payments to be spread over a period of years or creating special treatment for specific asset categories such as business assets. However, exceptions could undermine the purpose that many attach to a wealth tax: structuring the overall tax system to make all taxpayers pay their fair share.

Withholding Tax

What Is a Withholding Tax?

A withholding tax is the amount an employer withholds from an employee's wages and pays directly to the government. The amount withheld is a credit against the income taxes the employee must pay during the year. It also is a tax levied on income (interest and dividends) from securities owned by a nonresident alien, as well as other income paid to nonresidents of a country. Withholding tax is levied on most people who earn income from a trade or business in the United States.

Key Takeaways

- A withholding tax takes a set amount of money out of an employee's paycheck and pays it to the government.

- The money taken is a credit against the employee's annual income tax.

- If too much money is withheld, an employee will receive a tax refund; if not enough is withheld, an employee will have an additional tax bill.

Withholding Tax

Understanding Withholding Tax

Tax withholding is a way for the U.S. government to tax at the source of income, rather than trying to collect income tax after wages are earned. There are two diverse types of withholding taxes employed by the Internal Revenue Service (IRS) to ensure that proper tax is withheld in different situations.

U.S. Resident Withholding Tax

The first and more commonly discussed withholding tax is the one on U.S. residents' personal income that must be collected by every employer in the United States. Under the current system, the withholding tax is collected by employers and remitted directly to the government, with employees paying the remainder when they file a tax return in April each year.

If too much tax is withheld, it results in a tax refund. However, if not enough tax has been held back, then the individual owes money to the IRS.

You want about 90% of your estimated income taxes withheld by the government.5 It ensures that you never fall behind on income taxes, a failing that can carry heavy penalties, and it also sees to it that you are not overtaxed throughout the year. Investors and independent contractors are exempt from withholding taxes but not from income tax. (They are required to pay quarterly estimated tax.) If these classes of taxpayers fall behind, they can become liable to backup withholding, which is a higher rate of tax withholding, which is set at 24%.

You can easily perform a paycheck checkup using the IRS's tax withholding estimator. This tool helps identify the correct amount of tax withheld from each paycheck to make sure you do not owe more in April. Using the estimator will require your most recent pay stubs, your most recent income tax return, your estimated income during the current year, and other information.

Nonresident aliens who earn money in the U.S. are also subject to a withholding tax on that income.

Nonresident Withholding Tax

The other form of withholding tax is levied against nonresident aliens to ensure that proper taxes are made on income sources from within the United States. A nonresident alien is foreign-born and has not passed the green card test or a substantial presence test.

All nonresident aliens must file Form 1040NR if they are engaged in a trade or business in the United States during the year. If you are a nonresident alien, there are standard IRS deduction and exemption tables to help you figure out when you should be paying U.S. taxes and which deductions you may be able to claim.

History of Withholding Taxes

Tax withholding first occurred in the United States in 1862 at the order of President Abraham Lincoln to help finance the Civil War. The federal government also implemented excise taxes for the same purpose. Tax withholding and income tax were abolished after the Civil War in 1872.

The current system was accompanied by a large tax hike when it was implemented in 1943. At the time, it was thought that it would be difficult to collect taxes without getting them from the source. Most employees are subject to withholding taxes when they are hired and fill out a W-4 Form. The form estimates the amount of taxes that will be due.

The withholding tax is one of two types of payroll taxes. The other type is paid to the government by the employer and is based on an individual employee's wages. It is used to fund Social Security and federal unemployment programs (started by the Social Security Act of 1935) as well as Medicare (begun in 1966).

Special Considerations

U.S. states may also have state income taxes, and forty-one states and Washington, D.C., employ tax withholding systems to collect from their residents. States use a combination of the IRS W-4 Form and their own worksheets. Seven states—Alaska, Florida, Nevada, South Dakota, Texas, Washington, and Wyoming—do not charge income tax. New Hampshire and Tennessee do not tax wages but do tax dividends and income from investments. Both states voted to end this practice—Tennessee in 2021 and New Hampshire by 2025.

Now that you have an innovative idea about taxes, you know more than most people in business and more than the average lawyer. Do some calling, look around, interview, and always keep your business private, never talk about the money, it is no one business. Remember, you have a legal right to get your tax bill down, and you should, you are the one working all these sleepless nights.

WOW! Thank God that's over with. Truth be told, taxes do not need to be painful, however, they are. While it is almost impossible to cover everything here, the code book is over 1,000 pages. Use it! Get with a real good CPA, ask a lot of questions, about how to save on your taxes. And do tax planning too. See you at the bank, I will be the one smiling…

CPSIA information can be obtained
at www.ICGtesting.com
Printed in the USA
BVHW012140090223
658229BV00002B/2